STRIKE!

STRIKE!

THE FARM WORKERS' FIGHT FOR THEIR RIGHTS

Larry Dane Brimner

CALKINS CREEK
An Imprint of Highlights
Honesdale, Pennsylvania

In Spanish and English, strikers took to the picket lines.

FOR THOSE WHO HARVEST
THE FOOD FOR OUR TABLES,
AND FOR THE MIGRANT STUDENTS
I ONCE TAUGHT

—LDB

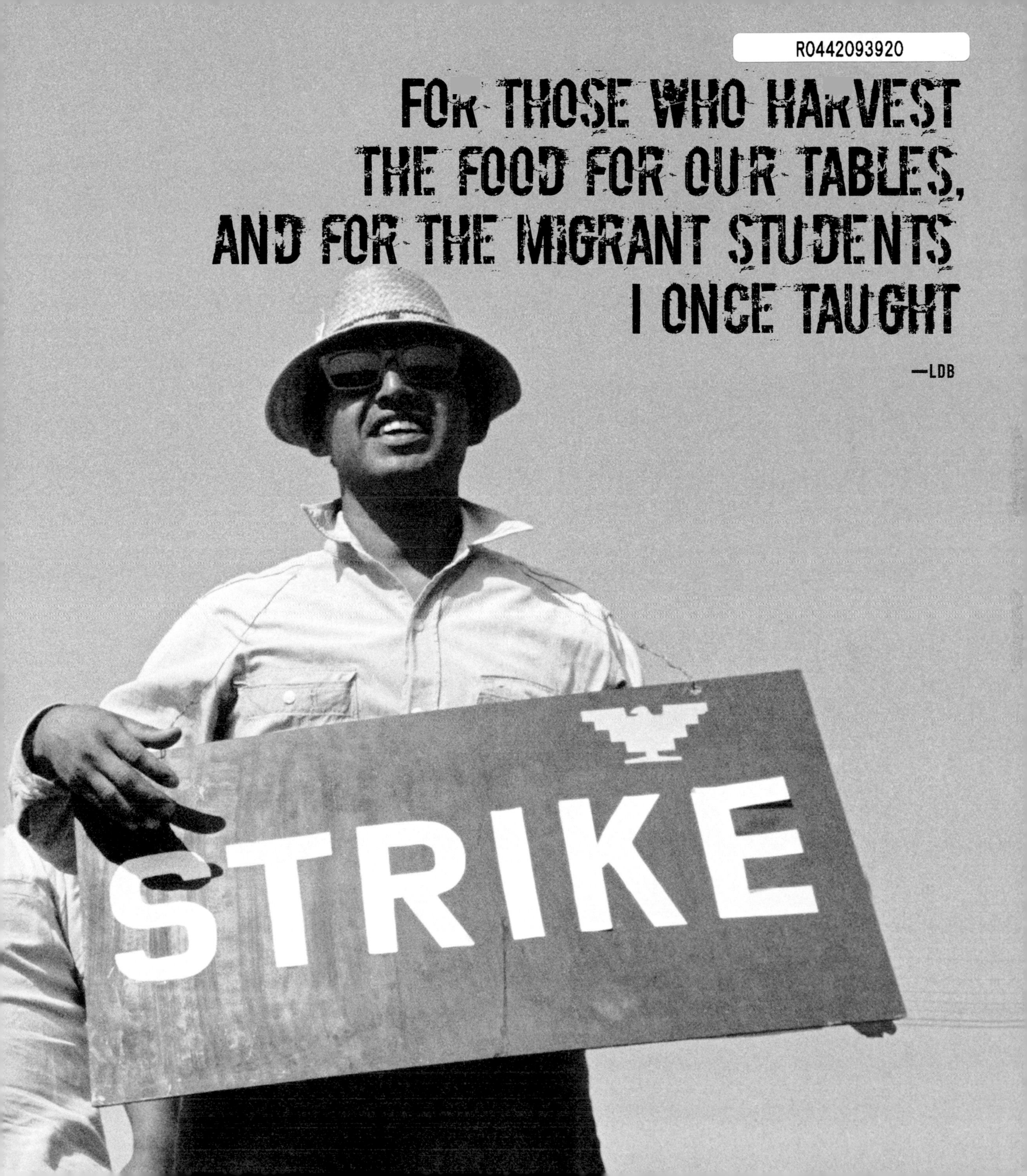

STRIKE

During the 1920s and '30s, farm workers tried to organize for better wages and work conditions. Here, a Mexican American picket line forms in Corcoran, California, in 1933.

CONTENTS

*Delano, el condado de Kern,
California, 1965*

Delano, Kern County,
California, 1965

OPPOSITE: *California's many crops feed the nation and the world.*

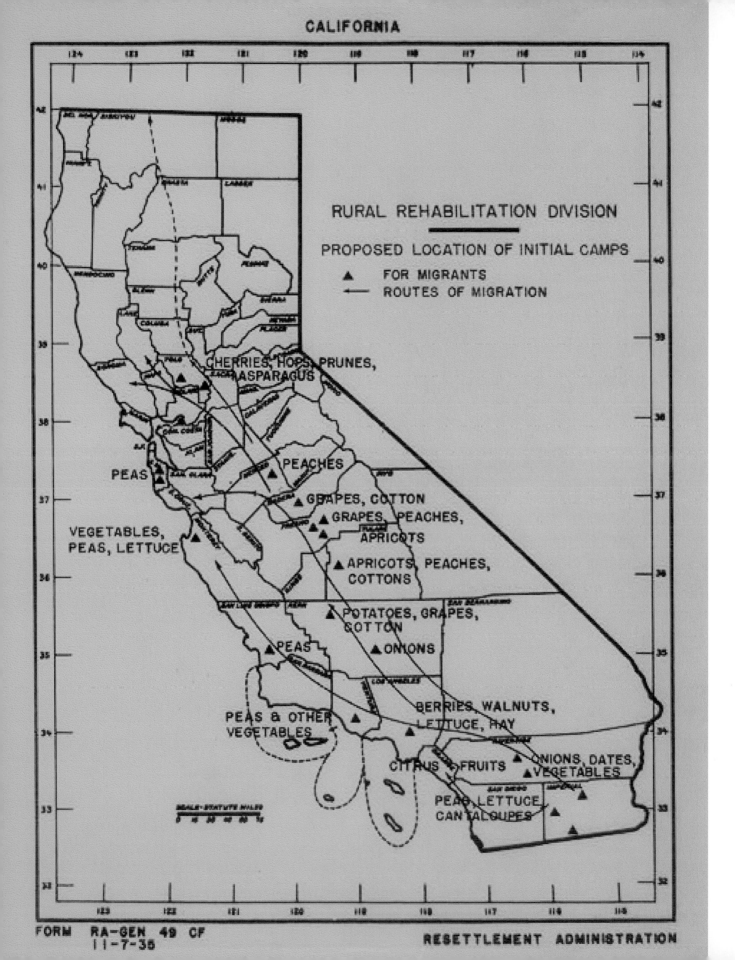

CALIFORNIA

RURAL REHABILITATION DIVISION

PROPOSED LOCATION OF INITIAL CAMPS

▲ FOR MIGRANTS
← ROUTES OF MIGRATION

CHERRIES, HOPS, PRUNES, ASPARAGUS

PEAS

PEACHES

VEGETABLES, PEAS, LETTUCE

GRAPES, COTTON

GRAPES, PEACHES, APRICOTS

APRICOTS, PEACHES, COTTONS

POTATOES, GRAPES, COTTON

PEAS

ONIONS

PEAS & OTHER VEGETABLES

BERRIES, WALNUTS, LETTUCE, HAY

CITRUS FRUITS

ONIONS, DATES, VEGETABLES

PEAS, LETTUCE, CANTALOUPES

SCALE-STATUTE MILES

La huelga de los trabajadores agrícolas Filipinos . . . comenzó esa mañana cuando los obreros abandonaron sus herramientas y las sustituyeron por pancartas.

The Filipino farm workers' strike . . . began that morning when workers exchanged their tools for picket signs.

Filipino workers pick lettuce in the Imperial Valley, a desert area east of San Diego and west of Yuma, Arizona.

SEPTEMBER 8, 1965, WAS NO ORDINARY DAY IN DELANO, CALIFORNIA.

The morning sun peeked over the Tehachapi Mountains some sixty-five miles east of this small town at the southern end of the state's Central Valley. It cast its warming rays on the area's vast agricultural fields. Almonds. Oranges. Asparagus. Cotton. And grapes: Thompson, Ribier, and Emperor, among other varieties. The grapevines in Delano's vineyards were heavy with fruit, ready to be harvested, boxed, and shipped to market. On a normal harvest day, these vineyards teemed with crews of Filipino farm workers, mostly single men, toiling among the vines. But on this September day, another story was told.

"FIELD STRIKE IDLES 1,000 IN KERN FIELDS."

The article in the *Fresno Bee* didn't tell the entire tale of the Filipino farm workers' strike that began that morning when workers exchanged their tools for picket signs to protest unfair wages and poor working and living conditions. The number of strikers varied, depending upon who was asked. "Growers say 500 workers are striking, but the Farm Labor Union says about 1,500 field-hands are out." The *Fresno Bee* settled on one thousand. Whatever their numbers, going out on strike—or refusing to work until their wage demands were met—had been an agonizing decision for these farm workers. They were the people who tended the crops and picked the food that ended up in kitchens and on tables across the United States and around the world. Year after year, the grape workers returned to the same vineyards as they followed the annual harvests that started in the irrigated southern deserts of California and moved northward into the fertile Central Valley.

A farm-labor camp in Texas offers only the basics.

The Delano grape workers wanted better wages. Growers paid them only 90¢ per hour, plus 10¢ per lug, or box, of grapes picked. At the end of the day, the average picker earned around $1.20 per hour, while some other farm workers were earning more. They also wanted better living conditions. Some of the Filipino workers lived in grower-provided labor camps. But often the housing in these camps was little more than corrugated metal or tar-paper shacks that were brutally harsh in cold weather and like furnaces in summer. Many of the camps lacked running water and indoor toilets. A dirty bathroom or single outhouse or two might serve all the workers living in each camp. It wasn't unusual for drinking and bathing water to come from a central spigot or from the open ditches used to irrigate the crops. Field hands might pay $2.00 or more per day for this housing, although a few growers provided it at no cost. Also, the money these workers earned during the harvest had to last throughout the rest of the year when jobs for seasonal laborers were few.

By walking off the job and striking, these workers faced permanent unemployment. Their bosses could blacklist them, putting their names on a list that would single them out as troublemakers. This would make them unemployable in the future. Even so, the Filipino grape pickers wanted growers to acknowledge that the work they did was difficult and required skill. They figured the best way for growers to show this was for them to pay wages equal to what other farm workers were earning. After all, many growers had become wealthy off the labor of field hands. Jim Smith of the International Brotherhood of Teamsters accused growers of "slave labor wages and conditions." He told members of the Agricultural Workers Organizing Committee (AWOC) at a mass meeting in Filipino Community Hall in Delano, "We're going to march up and down the San Joaquin Valley [Central Valley] and wake up the employers to the fact they have to pay union wages and provide union conditions. Now it's your turn to get the money, the growers have had it all these years." Indeed, workers wanted a fair share of the profits their labor

Larry Itliong immigrated to the United States in 1929 and almost immediately became involved in farm-labor issues. He helped found the Agricultural Workers Organizing Committee, settled wage disputes in the Coachella Valley, and led the 1965 Delano grape strike.

provided. Equally important, they wanted dignity and respect and were willing to face job loss and violence on picket lines to get it.

Months earlier, in May 1965, Larry Itliong, a Filipino farm worker and one of the leaders in AWOC, had negotiated better wages for grape pickers in the Coachella Valley. Often chomping on a cigar, he was known by his friends as "Seven Fingers." Stories about how he lost his fingers were numerous, but the factual details remained a mystery. Having only a sixth-grade education, Itliong was fifteen when he arrived in the United States in 1929. Like so many others who came to American shores, he hoped to find education and fortune. Instead, he found work in the lettuce fields of Washington State and, later, in the fish canneries of Alaska before joining the farm-labor force in California. Here, he followed the harvests of grapes, raisins, brussels sprouts, and other crops up and down the state. Unhappy with wages and working conditions in the Coachella Valley, a farming area located in the desert about 133 miles southeast of Los Angeles, he helped found AWOC in 1959. It was an outgrowth of the Agricultural Workers Association (AWA) and several earlier attempts to unionize field laborers. But organizing field hands was difficult since farm labor was migratory and seasonal. The workers moved from area to area as crops ripened and were ready for harvest. Previous efforts to enlist laborers into unions in the 1920s through the 1940s were crushed by growers, but not until they'd led to often violent, bloody, and deadly strikes. Workers were left disorganized and powerless against wealthy agricultural employers.

Itliong speaks with Brazilian farm laborers in the early 1960s.

THE *BRACERO* PROGRAM AND MEXICAN REPATRIATION

The Great Depression of the 1930s brought with it a campaign that is all but buried in history. During the Dust Bowl of this period, relentless drought and dust storms forced countless families to abandon their failed crops and worthless farms in the central and southern plains of the United States. A large number of these people headed to California. But their arrival resulted in a surplus of labor. As is often the case during hard economic times, people looked for someone to blame. Among those blamed for the unemployment, homelessness, and sour economy of the Great Depression were people of Mexican descent. Racial prejudice already existed against Mexicans and Mexican Americans, who often were willing to work for meager wages and at jobs that most white people, or Anglos, refused to do. With the arrival of the Dust Bowl refugees into California, more than enough workers were available to tend and harvest crops. Federal, state, and local government agencies began an anti-Mexican campaign between 1929 and 1939 to send hundreds of thousands of Mexicans and

Mexican Americans to Mexico. The program was called the Mexican Repatriation. However, *repatriation* means "to send back" or "to return." Many of those sent to Mexico were born in the United States and had never lived anywhere else. They were U.S. citizens, deprived of their citizenship.

When the U.S. entered World War II in December 1941, many farm workers joined the military or went to work in factories that supplied the war effort. Growers argued that field labor was in short supply because of the repatriation and war. President Franklin D. Roosevelt met with the Mexican president and agreed to a program of guest workers, the Mexican Farm Labor Program, commonly called the *bracero* program. Although few braceros, or "men who

work with their arms," actually entered the United States during the war, hundreds of thousands of them came after it ended.

· ·

Bracero *workers took jobs away from Americans. They also were abused by growers, who often threatened them with deportation if they didn't work hard enough or complained too much. Growers often cheated them out of wages they'd earned. The U.S. government, which failed to oversee the bracero program adequately, treated these foreign workers like cattle. In this photo, the workers are sprayed with DDT, a poisonous insecticide, upon entry into the country.*

16   STRIKE!

Yet, Itliong and others continued to believe that through their sheer numbers, workers could be a power equal to that of the growers if only they formed a union and stuck together to bargain with their bosses. It had worked with industrial employees and others. Why not with farm workers? And this newest union was different from those that had preceded it, and failed. In 1960, just one year after forming, AWOC got the financial backing of the American Federation of Labor and Congress of Industrial Organizations (AFL-CIO). This, the country's main alliance of independent unions, had joined together in the belief that a united work force was essential when bargaining with employers.

A year later, the alliance changed its relationship with AWOC. AFL-CIO president George Meany wrote to Eleanor Roosevelt, the former First Lady of the United States and a union supporter, that agricultural workers were happy to accept the raises AWOC negotiated but unwilling to become dues-paying members. He explained, "We have not been successful in building up membership to the point where we could look forward to a union which could sustain itself on the dues of its membership." Although he wasn't giving up on building a successful union of farm workers, he said the AFL-CIO needed to focus first on increasing its dues-paying members before tackling wages and working conditions.

By 1965, the alliance believed it had both a quantity of dues-paying members in AWOC and an issue it could take up: the California grape harvest.

California table grapes ripened first in the Coachella Valley. Because of this, growers there were able to demand top prices for their crop. When the Filipino workers arrived in the valley to harvest grapes, growers offered them only $1.25 per hour. Earlier, these growers had pressured their political allies to revive the *bracero* program that imported guest workers from Mexico. Although the program had officially ended in 1964, the administration of President Lyndon B. Johnson agreed to reinstate it on a limited basis. The California growers were

"La victoria . . .
no fue tanto para
el aumento de
salarios, sino por
su significado
de derrotar a los
productores."

....

"The victory was . . .
not so much for
the wage
increase but for
its significance at
defeating the
growers."

seeking low-wage workers for their fields through the bracero program. Instead, their plan backfired. The president's secretary of labor, W. Willard Wirtz, insisted that the guest workers be paid $1.40 per hour. Wirtz also required that growers make the jobs available to Americans first before requesting foreign field hands through the program. In the Coachella Valley, the Filipinos— all American citizens—demanded the wage that growers had agreed to pay the braceros. When the growers refused, Itliong and Ben Gines, another Filipino leader in AWOC, called for a strike. A reported one thousand "workers stayed off their jobs at several grape ranches" in the valley.

Violence quickly erupted between striking workers, growers, and strikebreakers, often called scabs. Arrests resulted: Gines "on charges of 'intimidation' on a picket line" and Vincente R. Alviar, a sixty-six-year-old striking grape picker, "on suspicion of battery after he allegedly struck a man trying to" enter a field to work.

It took ten days before growers agreed to pay the Filipinos the same wage as the braceros. Even then, the growers refused to admit the strike had brought them to the bargaining table. The Filipinos, though, viewed their success differently. "The victory [in the Coachella Valley] was . . . not so much for the wage increase but for its significance at defeating the growers," said Andy Imutan, also an AWOC leader, who was thirty-nine at the time of the Coachella Valley strike. He had only just emigrated from the Philippines to the United States with his wife earlier in 1965 and immediately got involved with labor issues. "We knew then that we could accomplish a lot more."

In September 1965, the Filipinos moved north to harvest grapes in the Delano-area vineyards. They asked for the same wage they'd been paid in May in the Coachella Valley. The growers offered them only $1.00 an hour. From the growers' perspective, it was time to show these workers who the bosses were.

Itliong sent letters to nine of the largest Delano grape growers, asking them to attend a meeting to discuss the situation. Not one bothered to respond. Not one bothered to attend.

Once again, he turned to the only tool at hand: STRIKE!

THE FILIPINO IN AMERICA

Following the end of the Spanish-American War, the United States, under President William McKinley (urged on by business leaders), took a strong interest in the Philippines as a stepping stone to exporting American goods to China. Although Filipino revolutionaries had declared independence from Spain on June 12, 1898, neither Spain nor the United States recognized that declaration. When the peace treaty was signed in December, ending the war, the United States officially took possession of the Philippines and Filipinos became U.S. citizens. But fighting continued until 1902 when rebels surrendered on the promise that independence eventually would be granted. The country didn't become a sovereign nation until July 4, 1946, when the United States granted it independence.

As U.S. citizens, Filipinos first were recruited by labor contractors to work in the sugarcane and pineapple fields of Hawaii, an American territory at the time. However, some plantation owners and contractors treated them harshly, at times whipping the Filipinos for not working hard enough.

Then in the late 1920s and 1930s—following the passage of the Immigration Act of 1924, which excluded Asians from entering the United States—more than one hundred thousand Filipinos, all American citizens and mostly young, single men, crossed the Pacific Ocean bound for the U.S. mainland. Here, they expected to get a good education, prosper, and return to the Philippines as wealthy gentlemen. But while some found work washing dishes or waiting tables in restaurants, most labored in the fields of American agriculture, where the pay was so poor that the men never earned enough money to return to their homeland. As farm worker Jacinto Sequig remembered, "I was surprised to find out that when I got to Seattle, there was no glittering gold or silver on the street where you could just pick it up and put it in your pocket. . . ." Instead, he went to work hoeing cabbages fifteen hours a day. "You know how much I was paid?" he asked an interviewer rhetorically. "One buck a day." And because laws in many states, including California, prohibited marriage between people of different races, the majority of these Filipino immigrants remained bachelors throughout their lives.

....

Although American citizens, Filipinos were forbidden by attitudes and laws from marrying outside their race. They often faced discrimination, and many were threatened.

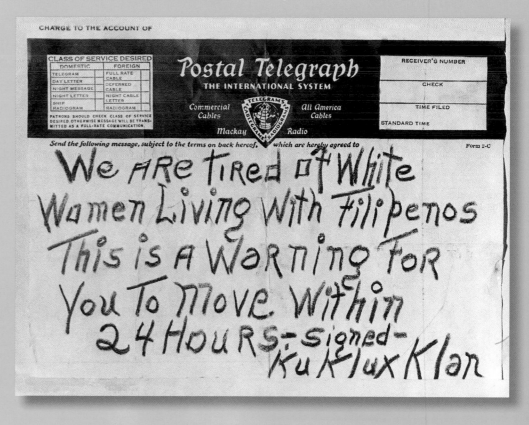

Filipinos en once ranchos más habían sumado al paro, convirtiéndolo en la huelga más grande de los viñedos de Delano desde la década de 1930.

....

Filipinos at eleven more ranches had joined the work stoppage, making it the biggest strike of Delano vineyards since the 1930s.

On the morning of September 8, 1965, instead of reporting to the fields to pick grapes, farm workers laid down their tools and refused to go to work. Some sat down beneath the grapevines and wouldn't budge. This disrupted laborers who did not join the strike, bringing work to a standstill. They first struck Lucas and Sons vineyard, but the strike quickly grew. By late morning, it included other ranches and more than a thousand workers. The striking grape pickers formed small picket lines at packing sheds and cold-storage plants, where grapes were put away for shipment later. Others carried handmade strike signs in front of vineyard entrances.

Californians already were reeling from racial riots in the Watts area of Los Angeles. On August 11, Lee W. Minkus, a white law-enforcement officer, stopped and arrested Marquette Frye, an African American man, on suspicion of driving while intoxicated. A crowd of onlookers gathered, and somebody pushed somebody else; it wasn't clear who started the scuffle. Minkus? Frye? Someone in the crowd? The onlookers began to throw rocks and bottles at Minkus, and when additional police arrived, a full-blown riot erupted. For six days, rioters in this mostly African American neighborhood overturned and set fire to automobiles and looted stores. People were frustrated by a lack of jobs and poor housing and schools, and Frye's arrest was the spark that set off the unrest. Now, less than 150 miles north of Los Angeles, tensions were growing in Delano's grape vineyards. It seemed as if the fabric of America was unraveling.

Joining Itliong and Imutan in the strike that September morning were other AWOC leaders. Philip Vera Cruz had come to the United States in 1926 at the age of twenty-two and worked in Alaskan fish canneries before becoming part of the California agricultural force. Pete Velasco had arrived in Los Angeles in 1931 from the Philippines and worked for a decade in area restaurants before joining the U.S. Army and serving in Europe during World War II. He returned after the war to do farm work.

But many other Filipino workers were reluctant at first to join the AWOC leaders. The laborers felt a kinship and loyalty to the

Itliong at his typewriter. Not only did he lead Filipino workers out of the vineyards, but he was also the voice and the main person to contact about the AFL-CIO– backed strike.

growers who hired them season after season, even if the growers didn't return this sentiment. The workers didn't want to antagonize their own bosses. So Itliong agreed that individuals didn't have to picket the vineyard where they worked. As a compromise, he said they could picket other vineyards. By that afternoon, Filipinos at eleven more ranches had joined the work stoppage, making it the biggest strike of Delano vineyards since the 1930s.

Workers would not harvest grapes that Wednesday in September. They vowed that they would not pick grapes again until their demands for higher wages were met. The workers knew that if the grapes were not harvested soon, they would ripen and rot on the vines.

A striking AWOC member on a road outside a grape vineyard

OPPOSITE: *Grapes and other crops grown in California ripen first in the fields of the southern deserts around Brawley and Coachella. As the harvest moves north, so do the workers.*

In "A Farm Worker's Viewpoint," Vera Cruz wrote, "The Filipino decision of the great Delano Grape Strike delivered the initial spark to explode the most brilliant incendiary bomb for social, economic and political changes in U.S. rural life. . . . It is . . . just against the law of nature that a few own everything and deny the right of a decent livelihood to others. This is what happened in Delano: the weak and oppressed of the land combined and fought the powerful for a just share of the harvest."

In American agriculture, growers had always dictated wages and offered little in the way of concern for their workers' needs. "Through the last one hundred years, California growers have grown accustomed to having as much labor as they wished, when they wished, for whatever purposes they wished, and under whatever conditions they wished. . . . That is to say, other industries have to offer wages, working conditions, and continuity of employment such as to attract and retain American workers. . . . Not so with California's industrialized agriculture." Growers didn't take the Delano grape strike seriously—at least not at first. Whenever complaints over wages or conditions had arisen in the past, they routinely set Filipinos against Mexicans and Mexican Americans (also known as Chicanos), and vice versa, as a way to keep wages low and to maximize their profits. Growers figured the Filipinos would get tired of carrying picket signs after a couple of days and return to work. And if they didn't, they could easily hire Mexican and Chicano workers to take their place.

After five days, however, the Filipinos had not returned to work. The growers began shutting off gas and electricity to the farm-labor camps, where many of the workers lived. Some padlocked strikers inside their housing to keep them from marching on picket lines, while other growers evicted their Filipino crews. Then they brought in buses of scabs to replace the striking workers. They took other actions as well. They went to court and got local judges to issue injunctions, or court orders. These injunctions limited the number of people who could picket and the number of places from which they could appeal to workers who were still in the vineyards. Growers sought, and won,

restrictions on the amount of noise that strikers could make, which prevented protesters from using bullhorns to call out to strikebreakers in the fields. When strikers violated the injunctions, local police officers or sheriff's deputies arrested them.

Both Itliong and Imutan were aware of the tactics that growers traditionally used to break strikes. Imutan explained, "Mexican workers started crossing our picketlines. There was no unity between the Mexicans and the Filipinos. The growers were very successful in dividing us and creating conflict between the two races. Although we tried to discourage and reason with the Mexicans that this was just hurting everyone, we weren't able to convince them." Everyone knew the strike would fail if Mexicans and Chicanos continued to cross the Filipinos' picket lines to work in the struck vineyards. Pete Velasco put it this

"Si no implica a todos los demás . . . para estar con usted, usted fracasara."

"If you don't involve all the others . . . to be with you, you are sunk."

way: "There are Mexicans, there are whites, and there are blacks and if you don't involve all the others . . . to be with you, you are sunk . . . because those . . . that are not involved become your scabs . . . and they break your strike."

Itliong and Imutan turned to César Chávez who, along with Dolores Huerta and others, was slowly building the National Farm Workers Association (NFWA) into an organization to improve the lives of Mexican and Chicano farm laborers. Unlike AWOC, it had little money and no backing from organized labor. Chávez believed his infant organization wasn't ready to get involved in a strike. But Itliong and the other AWOC leaders persisted, calling on Chávez several times to ask him to bring the NFWA into the Filipino strike. Finally, Chávez's wife, Helen, and Huerta pressed him to let the struggling union's members make the decision.

OPPOSITE: *Larry Itliong and other Filipino members of AWOC started the Delano grape strike when they demanded to be paid the same as foreign guest workers.*

La tierra

....

Soil

During the Dust Bowl, families from the central and southern plains of the United States migrated through Arizona on their way to California, hoping for a better life.

STATE OF ARIZONA

BEST COPY
AVAILABLE

SUPPLEMENT ATTACHED

ARIZONA STATE BOARD OF HEALTH

BUREAU OF VITAL STATISTICS
ORIGINAL CERTIFICATE OF BIRTH

State Index No. *594*
County Registrar No.
Local Registrar No. *75*

PLACE OF BIRTH
y of *Yuma*
f. *Yuma*
Yuma

North Gila Valley No. _____ St. _____ Ward
(If birth occurred in a hospital or institution, give its NAME instead of street and number)

name of child *Caesario Chavez*

(If child is not yet named, make supplemental report, as directed)

of Child | To be answered ONLY in event of plural births. | 4. Twin, triplet or other _____ | 6. Legitimate? *Yes* | 7. Date of birth *Mar-31-27* Month Day Year

5. No., in order of birth *1*

FATHER		14. MOTHER
name *Lebrodo Chavez*		Full maiden name *Jucosa Estroda*
residence (Usual place of abode) *Yuma Ariz*		15 Residence (Usual place of abode) *Yuma Ariz*
non-resident, give place and state.		If non-resident, give place and state.
Color of race *Mexican*	11. Age at last birthday *38* (Years)	16 Color or race *Mexican*	17. Age at last birthday *25* (Years)
Birthplace (city or place) *Mexico* (State or country)		18. Birthplace (city or place) *Mexico* (State or country)
Occupation *Farmer* Nature of industry		19. Occupation *Housewife* Nature of industry

Number of children of this mother taken at time of birth of child herein certified and including this child.
(a) Born alive and now living *7*
(b) Born alive but now dead *2*
(c) Stillborn

21. Were precautions taken against ophthalmia neonatorum? *Yes*

CERTIFICATE OF ATTENDING PHYSICIAN OR MIDWIFE*
hereby certify that I attended the birth of this child, who was *alive* at *3* m. on the date above stated
(Born alive or stillborn.)

* When there was no attending physician or midwife, then the father, householder, etc. should make this return. A stillborn child is one that neither breathes nor shows other evidence of life after birth.

Signature *H D Ketchenede — M D*
(Physician or midwife).
Address *Yuma Ariz*

Filed *April 1,* 1927 *H. Chipperman Deputy* Local Registrar

Given name added from supplemental report, _____ Month, day, year

Filed _____, 19 _____ County Registrar

Registrar

339-331-151

7/15/2013

This is a true certification of the facts on file with the OFFICE OF VITAL RECORDS, ARIZONA DEPARTMENT OF HEALTH SERVICES, PHOENIX, ARIZONA Revised 12/2012.

KHALEEL HUSSAINI
ASSISTANT STATE REGISTRAR

This copy not valid unless prepared on a form displaying the State Seal and impressed with the raised seal of the issuing agency.

C8085739

Arizona
Department of
Health Services

ANY ALTERATION OR ERASURE VOIDS THIS DOCUMENT

THE SECOND OF LIBRADO AND JUANA CHÁVEZ'S FIVE CHILDREN, CÉSARIO ESTRADA CHÁVEZ, CALLED CÉSAR, CAME TO THE NFWA FROM THE SOIL.

Born in the northern Gila River Valley outside Yuma, Arizona, on March 31, 1927, young Chávez grew up in a small adobe farmhouse on a ranch that his paternal grandfather had homesteaded several years before Arizona became a state in 1912. His grandfather spilled his sweat on the rich soil, brought water to it, and carved an oasis out of the small plot of land not far from the Colorado River. The river provided the ranch with irrigation. For Chávez, the ranch was an idyllic place with an abundance of watermelons, chili peppers, and sweet corn to eat and a surplus of nearby cousins with whom to play—"at least 180 . . . , many of those already married and with families of their own." Even with the onset of the Great Depression, when hundreds of thousands of Americans were homeless and stood in lines for food, Chávez's family had a comfortable place to live. They also grew enough food to share with others. Despite this, he remembered, "Our need for money was obvious. . . . [So my brother] Richard and I started trapping gophers for the irrigation district." The rodents would burrow into the walls of the canals, causing them to weaken and collapse. When the pair found a gopher in one of their traps, they'd cut off its tail and feed the rest of it to several of "the fattest cats in the world," which followed them around.

"*Para mí la base tiene que ser la fe.*"

....

"For me the base must be faith."

"For each tail we received a penny." Although they had little money and few store-bought products, the Chávezes were spared many of the difficulties facing much of the rest of the country.

Chávez's mother, a gentle, devoutly religious woman, shaped the way he looked at life. Raised a Catholic, he recalled, "It was my mother who taught us prayers" and proverbs, or *dichos*. She often told him he was given a mind and a tongue to get out of situations without raising his fists. She taught him compassion and concern by sending him and Richard out to look for hobos and those who were less fortunate to invite home for a meal. Sometimes these visitors "would offer to do some work, like chop wood, in exchange for [the] meal, but [his mother] would refuse because, she said, the gift then was invalid" in God's eyes. While it was his mother who taught the children their prayers, it was his paternal grandmother who taught them the Catholic catechism, a brief summary of Christianity through questions and answers. She had prepared Chávez and his sister Rita so well that their priest said they could take their first Communion without formal instruction. "Since those days," Chávez said years later, "my need for religion has deepened. Today I don't think that I could base my will to struggle on cold economics or on some political doctrine. I don't think there would be enough to sustain me. For me the base must be faith."

The year Chávez turned ten, his idyllic life at his grandfather's ranch began to change. The Colorado River slowed to a trickle. The canals that delivered water to their ranch ran dry. Trees and crops wilted and withered.

The drought brought even more hardship. Chávez's father, who now worked the farm, owed more than $4,000 in back property taxes and was unable to pay. The bank took possession of the farm in August 1937, and a year later his father joined the Dust Bowl refugees in California.

The elder Chávez found work in Oxnard, a seaside community north of Los Angeles, where he threshed beans, or separated them from their hulls. He found a modest house to live in and sent word for his family to join him.

Many Dust Bowl refugees crossed the Colorado River at Yuma into the agricultural fields of California's Imperial Valley.

In Oxnard, the entire family worked. The children attended school only part of the time so they could help. On weekends, they picked walnuts with their parents. If they could manage to save enough to pay the debt on the farm near Yuma, there was a chance they might be able to return to it for good. However, field workers were easy to come by and growers, knowing this, paid them very little. So desperate were the Chávezes that they sometimes searched for wild mustard greens in order to have food to eat. They earned barely enough to put gas into their old Studebaker and limp to the next job or crop that needed harvesting or tending. They were penniless when they returned to the Yuma-area farm a few months later in a last attempt to save it. But even their many relatives, now caught up in the Great Depression themselves, were unable to help.

Fue trabajar en los campos de lechuga . . . lo que causó una impresión duradera en Chávez.

....

It was working in the lettuce fields . . . that made a lasting impression on Chávez.

On February 6, 1939, a legal notice appeared in the local Yuma paper. The county was putting the Chávez homestead up for auction to settle the taxes that were due on it. The notice said nothing of Chávez's grandfather "who plowed the land, irrigated it, and made it produce. Nor did it mention [Chávez's] dad who had continued the work and struggled there for the survival of his family." Within weeks, the homestead sold. There was nothing left for the Chávezes to do except jam what few belongings they could into the old Studebaker and leave Arizona for good. The day they left, Chávez's father had only $40 in his pocket from the sale of a few chickens and cows.

Uprooted and with no place to call home, Chávez and his family now were migrants set adrift. Years later, Chávez recalled that day when the tractor came to tear up the soil, plowing under trees and destroying what three generations of Chávezes had nurtured, the day their lives were turned upside down: "God writes in exceedingly crooked lines."

Over the next decade, the family would toil in fields belonging to others. He recalled that one of their first jobs was picking peas at 20¢ for a twenty-five pound hamper. The whole family worked. After three hours, they'd made only about 20¢. It was working in the lettuce fields, however, that made a lasting impression on Chávez. He recalled that the crop had to be thinned using a short-handled hoe only twenty-four inches long that required workers to bend at the waist for hours at a time. Called *el cortito* ("the short one"), the hoe was awkward and painful to use. It left workers with long-lasting physical injuries. Chávez said using it was like being nailed to a cross. He quickly learned that toiling on land belonging to others wasn't the same as working on the family homestead. Although they and other farm workers harvested California's abundant crops, they were paid so poorly that most couldn't afford to purchase the food they'd picked. By necessity, Chávez and his two brothers and two sisters worked alongside their parents as they crisscrossed the state, following one harvest after another. It took every hand to put food on their table and a roof over their heads, even when

Agricultural-camp housing provided little shelter from the extremes of heat and cold in the desert regions of the Imperial and Coachella Valleys.

Chávez had only an eighth-grade education when he left school for good. But he continued to educate himself by reading books and articles.

that roof was nothing more than a leaky tent or a miserable farm-labor camp shed.

Eventually, the family heard that they could earn some money in San Jose, southeast of San Francisco, picking cherries and apricots. They settled in a *barrio*, or neighborhood, that local residents called *Sal Si Puedes*. It means "Get out if you can." The San Jose barrio was a small, rough neighborhood with occasional fistfights breaking out on its dirt roads. It became home for a brief period of time until the Chávezes picked up and moved again to the next crop, the next California harvest. Despite the moves and the fact that the Chávez children often worked alongside their parents, Chávez's mother insisted that her children go to school. He remembered that she would say, "'I didn't learn, but you can learn, so you have to go.'" And the children did go, but "school was just a nightmare" for young Chávez. He recalled having his knuckles rapped with a ruler for speaking Spanish, which was the language he spoke at home. Over the years, he and Richard attended more than thirty schools. In 1942, at the age of fifteen, he graduated eighth grade. His father had been injured recently in an automobile accident. Because Chávez did not want his mother to work any longer in the fields, he left school to join the ranks of migrant farm workers full time.

After leaving school, he briefly rebelled and flirted with being a *pachuco*—a flashy dresser. Pachucos were known for wearing peg-legged pants, long coats, lengthy key chains, and flat, broad-rimmed hats. Because their appearance made them stand out, they often became the targets of the police and others. Chávez liked to point out, though, that he "didn't affect the key chain, or the hat."

It was during his pachuco period that he met Helen Fabela, a student at Delano High School. She recalled, "César used to migrate and come by Delano every year. One day we were at a little sno-cone parlor . . . and listening to music when he came in with some other people. That's when I met him." The two began taking in an occasional movie or going to a dance. But their

A pachuco in long coat, peg-legged pants, and flat hat awaits booking into jail. Because of the way they dressed, pachucos stood out and often got involved in fights with sailors and others. Arrests of the pachucos followed, whether or not they were at fault.

"It [was] worse than being in prison. And there was lots of discrimination."

friendship was interrupted, first while Chávez followed the crops and then when, in 1946 at the age of nineteen, he joined the U.S. Navy. He described his time in the Navy as "the worst of my life: this regimentation, this super authority that somehow somebody has the right to move you around like a piece of equipment. It [was] worse than being in prison. And there was lots of discrimination." He served in the Navy for two years and then returned to migrant work. He also resumed his friendship with Fabela. The couple married on October 22, 1948, in Reno, Nevada.

He picked cotton the first winter they were married, but after that he was unable to find field work. He explained, "The braceros took all those jobs, and we [Chicanos] couldn't get them anymore." The couple moved to the San Jose barrio of Sal Si Puedes. San Jose was California's second-largest center of Mexican Americans after Los Angeles. It appealed to him, too, because Richard had found work there as an apprentice carpenter. He helped Chávez get a job at a local lumber mill.

While living in San Jose, Chávez met Fred Ross, a man who changed the direction of his life. Ross was born in San Francisco and trained as a teacher, but he was unable to find a teaching job during the Depression. Instead, he was hired as a social worker and later by the Farm Security Administration (FSA), a federal agency that tried to improve the lives of rural Americans. It was with the FSA in California that Ross first saw the poverty field hands faced. Many of them were transplants from the Dust Bowl or Mexican Americans, and he encouraged them to band together to improve their own lives. After World War II, he helped found the Community Service Organization (CSO) in 1947 with the goal of improving the lives of Mexican Americans through voter registration drives, English and citizenship classes, and civic action. The CSO believed change would come through the ballot box with the election of sympathetic politicians.

Ross, an Anglo, heard about Chávez and his wife from a Catholic parish priest, Father Donald McDonnell. Chávez often went with the priest to the fields to perform Mass and talk with laborers about their problems. After Ross's first meeting with

Chávez in 1952, he convinced the former migrant worker to volunteer for the CSO. He found Chávez to be a hard worker, an excellent organizer, and someone who could speak to farm workers because he'd labored in the fields himself.

Chávez's volunteer status soon ended, though, when Ross hired Chávez as a full-time organizer for the CSO at $35 a week. It was far more than he was earning at the San Jose lumber mill. In Ross, Chávez found a lifelong friend and mentor.

Chávez barreled into his new job, working night and day to sign up Mexican American residents in the biggest voter registration drive Sal Si Puedes had ever seen. With the help of Richard and friends, he registered thousands of people. Chávez organized similar voter registration drives among Mexican Americans while setting up new CSO chapters in the Central Valley. He was so successful at registering new voters, however, that some people began to fear Mexican Americans would control California elections. These individuals started a rumor that Chávez and the CSO were Communist agents. Communism is the opposite of America's capitalist system, in which property and goods are owned by individuals. Communists believe all private property should be eliminated and, instead, owned by the community or state.

Being called a Communist or sympathizer of Communism, whether true or not, could ruin a person's reputation and career in the United States. It could even result in being sent to prison. When a local district attorney accused Chávez of being a Communist, the CSO organizer stood up to the charge. He knew the majority of Mexican Americans were devout Catholics, so he asked Father McDonnell and other priests to speak on his behalf. This quieted the issue for the time.

In 1955, three years after Chávez went to work for the CSO, another young, energetic Mexican American also joined: Dolores Huerta. Born on April 10, 1930, in the small coal-mining town of Dawson, New Mexico, she arrived in Stockton, California, at the age of three after her parents' divorce. Her mother, Alicia Chávez Fernández, was a strong, independent businesswoman. She saved the money she earned as a waitress and bought a restaurant and hotel that catered to farm workers. She taught Huerta compassion by example. She often allowed laborers to stay for free in the hotel or to pay when they could. Huerta learned early that men and women could do the same jobs. She and her two brothers did the same chores at home. Her father, with whom she remained close, taught her to respect the labor of others. Serving in New Mexico's state legislature, he was a union activist and fought for laws to protect workers. After graduating high school in 1947, Huerta attended college briefly but left to marry her high-school sweetheart in 1950. After the marriage ended in 1953 and now responsible for herself and two daughters, she returned to college to earn a teaching degree. Although she had never experienced field work firsthand, she knew of the injustices and terrible working conditions farm laborers faced from those who stayed in her mother's hotel. After teaching a year and tired of seeing her students come to school hungry and shoeless, she left in search of something that would allow her to have more impact on farm workers' children. She believed she'd found it in Fred Ross's CSO.

SAUL ALINSKY AND THE COMMUNITY SERVICE ORGANIZATION

Although the Community Service Organization (CSO) was founded in 1947 by activist Fred Ross, he took his lead from Saul Alinsky. Ross was a student and an admirer of Alinsky's, who in the late 1930s and 1940s began a network of grassroots community organizations aimed at giving political voice and power to the voiceless. He started in the slums of Chicago, his hometown, and quickly expanded to African American ghetto areas across the nation. Nonviolent by nature, Alinsky believed in confrontational politics. His strategy was to bait the establishment through mass protest marches, strikes, boycotts, sit-ins, and sit-downs to shed light on existing problems in an effort to get them remedied. He believed such acts and the establishment's often violent reaction to them would draw attention to injustices people faced and grow popular support. Many credit him with laying the foundation for tactics—nonviolent but confrontational—that were used in the modern civil rights movement of the 1950s and 1960s. He described his book *Rules for Radicals* as a guide for the less fortunate and downtrodden to take power away from the high and mighty. With the CSO, Ross borrowed Alinsky's ideas to focus attention on police brutality and discrimination against Mexican Americans. In a similar way, Chávez used them to highlight the deplorable working and living conditions of the American farm worker.

Dolores Huerta and Larry Itliong in the 1970s. Both helped found the Agricultural Workers Organizing Committee.
The individual in the middle is unidentified.

While with the CSO, Huerta first raised funds and conducted voter registration drives. But she soon began to lobby legislators in Sacramento, the state capital, meeting with them personally and persuading them to pass bills that benefited Mexican Americans. Her efforts as a lobbyist while at the CSO resulted in the passage of laws ranging from allowing Spanish-language driver's license exams to old-age pension benefits for immigrants.

When Huerta met Chávez through Fred Ross and the CSO in 1956, she expected him to be dynamic and forceful because of his reputation as an outstanding organizer among other CSO workers. Instead, she found him to be extremely quiet. By working with him over the next couple of years, she discovered that the praise Ross and others heaped upon Chávez as a leader and organizer was well deserved.

WE SERVE WHITE'S only
NO
SPANISH or MEXICANS

Like Filipinos and other Asians, Mexicans and Mexican Americans, or Chicanos, faced much of the same discrimination that hurt African Americans in the United States.

In 1958, Huerta helped Father Thomas McCullough form the Agricultural Workers Association (AWA). McCullough quickly complained to the AFL-CIO, the powerful labor alliance, that it had ignored agricultural workers in favor of the industrial force. Embarrassed, the AFL-CIO decided the next year to back the organization financially, and the Agricultural Workers Organizing Committee was formed. Itliong joined AWOC as a paid organizer. Like Itliong, most of the organization's members were Filipino

Chávez . . . conocía los riesgos y los obstáculos que encontraría la organización de un sindicato para los trabajadores agrícolas.

Chávez . . . knew the risks and the long odds against successfully organizing a union for farm workers.

Americans. Although AWOC won some wage increases from growers, it failed to attract many Mexican American field hands to its membership rolls. Mexican Americans made up the majority of agricultural workers in California. There was still distrust between these two groups of field laborers from past decades, when growers used one race to break the strikes and defeat the union-organizing efforts of the other.

Frustrated by the continuing poverty and harsh conditions that agricultural workers faced, Chávez wanted to build a farm-labor union straight from the fields. He knew the history of the previous one hundred years: every union that tried to organize field laborers failed. Most of those unions had been led and supported by union leaders who were not farm workers. Chávez was convinced that for an agricultural union to be successful, it had to be organized from the ground up: by farm workers for farm workers. Building an organization that would benefit people in the fields had been a dream since he had his first taste of the impoverished life of a migrant worker. His wife commented, "César had always talked about organizing farm workers, even before CSO." At first, he tried to convince the CSO to support his efforts at building such an organization, but the leadership had shifted its emphasis to the cities where Chicanos were fighting discrimination and police brutality. So on March 31, 1962, his thirty-fifth birthday, Chávez abruptly quit the CSO to start a union of and by migrant workers.

Upon learning that Chávez had left the CSO, Norman Smith, the Anglo assistant director of AWOC, offered him a job. Chávez turned it down. He didn't think the AFL-CIO would give him the freedom he wanted to run things his own way. "My only hope of success was if no strings were attached," he explained.

Chávez and his wife knew the risks and the long odds against successfully organizing a union for farm workers. Now without an income, he moved his family to Delano, where his wife's relatives lived. He knew they would not let his family starve. Also, his brother Richard was now a carpenter and had relocated to Delano. He would help Chávez if he needed it. The former

migrant worker and CSO organizer rented the cheapest house he could find, where he set up an office. With only about $1,200 in life savings, Chávez knew it would be difficult to build a union from the ground up and that life would be tough and full of sacrifice for his wife and children, now numbering eight. Within days, however, the National Farm Workers Association was open for business.

Chávez, with his youngest children piled in the backseat of his car, drove to farm towns up and down California's Central Valley trying to recruit field hands into his infant union. It was a tough sell. He would talk to one hundred workers before finding one or two willing to join. Often he would return home discouraged after fruitless days on the road, having recruited no one.

His reputation as a capable organizer for CSO had spread in political circles far beyond California. In 1962, President John F. Kennedy's administration offered him a position with the Peace Corps in Latin America. The Peace Corps was a federal program of Americans who volunteered to foreign countries to assist in education, community and health programs, or whatever the host country thought it needed. While volunteers aided the country they were assigned to, they also improved the image of the United States abroad. Taking the position with the Peace Corps would have meant economic stability and given his children many advantages. But, like the job with AWOC, Chávez turned it down. His wife backed him one hundred percent, as did his friend and mentor, Fred Ross.

Founding the union was a leap of faith, and not just because the odds were against its success. He still had serious doubts that he would succeed. Still, Chávez continued because he believed it was his calling.

Helen and César with six of their eight children (circa 1969). They are Anna, Eloise, and Sylvia (standing from the left); and Paul, Elizabeth, and Anthony (seated from the left). Not pictured are Fernando and Linda.

Los campesinos

....

Peasants

OPPOSITE: *Agricultural workers—men, women, and children—toil beneath a blazing sun to turn California's barren land into rich, productive fields.*

The union's eagle symbol was purposely simple so that anyone could reproduce it.

AT FIRST, CHÁVEZ INTENDED FOR THE NATIONAL FARM WORKERS ASSOCIATION (NFWA) TO BE A UNION IN EVERYTHING BUT NAME.

Among field laborers, unions conjured up strikes and the growers' brutality when crushing them. Workers who were seen as troublemakers, who complained too much, or who were thought to be someone who might stir up a strike in the fields found that growers would blacklist them. Unions also had shown little success against the corporate farm structure in California. Chávez explained, "The power of the growers was backed by the power of the police, the courts, state and federal laws, and the financial power of the big corporations." Past unions may have won wage increases on occasion. However, these victories were usually temporary and had done nothing to address working and living conditions and had not resulted in contracts and job security. Chávez wanted to do more for farm workers than temporarily increase their wages. He shied away from calling his organization a union, as had AWOC. He didn't want to face defeat even before he'd begun.

The first thing he did was draw a map by hand of all the towns in the Central Valley, from Stockton in the north to Arvin in the south. Then he drove. "I just drove by myself for two and a half days, looking around, crisscrossing the valley," he said. He'd stop along the way to ask questions of workers. Were they making enough? How were they being treated?

Eventually, he started holding meetings in workers' houses, a tactic he'd learned from Ross. He found that people were more

Los trabajadores pensaron que tendrían pocas posibilidades de éxito contra productores que eran ricos, poderosos, y con conexiones políticos.

....

Workers thought that they stood little chance of success against growers, who were rich, powerful, and politically connected.

relaxed and their answers more forthright during these house meetings than when he approached workers in the fields, where a foreman or supervisor or labor contractor might overhear them. In the fields, most field hands usually wouldn't endorse the idea of organizing, but in the privacy of their houses they thought it might be a good thing. At the same time, the majority of these workers thought that they stood little chance of success against growers, who were rich, powerful, and politically connected.

Chávez was just another worker to the Chicano laborers in the fields. They identified with him, and he with them. While Chávez was recruiting and organizing members, Helen supported the family. "I was picking grapes or doing whatever field work was available," she said. "When the grape harvest was pretty heavy, sometimes I'd work ten hours a day, five days a week, for eighty-five cents an hour." Sometimes the older children would help her on weekends, if they weren't helping Chávez distribute union leaflets up and down the valley. His children often acted as his crew, canvassing the valley with him to persuade farm workers to join the new union.

By September 1962, Chávez believed they were ready to hold a founding convention. He set the date of Sunday, September 30, at an abandoned movie theater in Fresno. Richard designed a bold symbol for the fledgling organization: a black eagle—after the one on the Mexican flag—set in a white circle against a red field. The wings of the eagle were created with straight lines so it would be easy for people to draw by hand. The colors were symbolic. Black represented the plight of the workers, while white stood for their hope. Red signified the sacrifices people would have to make in order to get what they wanted. Chávez also explained, "Red and black flags are used for strikes in Mexico."

And what did the NFWA want for farm workers? It wanted to lobby in Sacramento for a minimum wage of $1.50 an hour and unemployment insurance. It also wanted the right to negotiate with growers about pay, working conditions, and other protections. Because of lobbying by wealthy growers, especially in the South, where most field laborers were African American, agricultural

At the NFWA founding convention, Chávez was elected president and Huerta a vice president. Here they stand with two unidentified convention attendees.

workers had been excluded from the National Labor Relations Act of 1935. This law allowed factory employees to organize and form unions to negotiate with their employers but ignored farm hands. The federal act also excluded maids and housekeepers, who were largely African American. In the fields, many growers still charged workers for drinking water, a quarter a cup. Some provided an old tin can from which all the workers drank. Rest breaks were unheard of. And toilet facilities in the fields were rare, leaving workers—male and female—to seek out whatever privacy they could find. By the end of the founding convention,

the delegates—mostly Mexican Americans—wholeheartedly embraced the NFWA's agenda. They also unanimously adopted Richard's flag as their symbol and *¡Viva la Causa!*—Long Live the Cause!—as their official motto. Membership dues of $3.50 a month would help support the union's efforts. The members elected Chávez to be their president, and Huerta, Gilbert Padilla, and Julio Hernandez as vice presidents. Padilla and Hernandez were Chávez's friends—Padilla from the CSO—and had been instrumental in recruiting members to the NFWA.

Over the next three years, the association struggled along, but Chávez, Huerta, Padilla, Hernandez, and the others who began the NFWA had a clear vision of what they wanted it to be. They knew it would take more than a union to overcome the poverty and discrimination farm laborers faced. It would take a movement—one that addressed these and other crippling issues field workers confronted in farm communities. Even before there were any union contracts, Chávez organized people by providing them with services: a credit union, a modest death-benefit plan, and a gas station for workers. To start the credit union, Chávez convinced Richard to use his Delano house as security against a bank loan.

The union began publication of a newspaper in December 1964. *El Malcriado* was the voice of farm workers and meant, in English, "ill-bred" or "children who speak back to their parents." The newspaper called for living wages and reported about field conditions that laborers had to endure. It made fun of wealthy growers and was an instant hit with workers. But labor contractors—middlemen who hired laborers on behalf of farm owners—and Delano growers were far less amused.

Chávez continued to drive his old station wagon up and down the valley, attracting new members to grow the union. Huerta, Padilla, and Hernandez also worked tirelessly to make the NFWA successful. Like Chávez, Huerta enlisted her children to go door-to-door with her to help pass out union information.

Finally, the NFWA organized its first strike in March 1965 in McFarland, a small farming community south of Delano.

Workers in the flower industry there had to crawl for hours on their hands and knees to tend fields of roses. It was a job that demanded sharp skills and experience, but growers refused to honor the wage they'd promised. Although Chávez didn't think the NFWA could organize a picket line, he did get some of the workers at McFarland's biggest rose grower to agree to stay home from work. At one point, though, Huerta had to use her truck and hide its keys to block a group of men from leaving their driveway and reporting to the fields. The grower quickly brought in strikebreakers from Mexico, but they were unskilled at working in the roses. After three days, he was eager to win back his experienced crew and agreed to pay them what he had promised.

Los delegados . . . aprobaron por unanimidad . . .¡Viva la Causa!—¡Larga vida a la causa!— como su lema oficial.

The delegates . . . unanimously adopted . . . *¡Viva la Causa!—* Long Live the Cause!—as their official motto.

As far as Chávez was concerned, the battle in the rose fields of McFarland was a minor victory. The strike boosted morale and had won workers their promised wage, but it achieved no contract or guarantees for the future. He reasoned it would still be some time before the NFWA was ready to take on California's agribusinesses, the large farms owned by corporations, in any real and significant way.

OPPOSITE: *Despite long hours and hard work, field hands often could not afford to feed their families the food they had harvested.*

Las uvas

······························

Grapes

Laborers empty lugs of harvested grapes during the California strike.

BY SEPTEMBER 1965, THE NFWA HAD ABOUT TWELVE HUNDRED MEMBERS; HOWEVER, ONLY TWO HUNDRED WERE PAYING MEMBERSHIP DUES.

OPPOSITE: *Chávez on a picket line in the 1960s*

Although Itliong and the other Filipino leaders asked him several times to join AWOC's strike, Chávez repeatedly refused. Years later, he explained his reluctance to join the strike by saying, "I thought the growers were powerful and arrogant . . . but I wasn't afraid of them or their power. I was afraid of the weakness of the people." He worried that the NFWA wouldn't be able to support its members financially if it honored AWOC's strike. If it couldn't, then surely they would cross the Filipino picket lines for work. Even so, with his wife and Huerta pressing him to let the NFWA's membership speak for itself, he set a date for a strike-vote meeting.

Itliong and some of the other Filipino leaders saw Chávez's hesitation as something else: ego. They were angered by his lack of immediate support. Indeed, some didn't understand his need for an organization separate from AWOC. These individuals began to view him as a competitor rather than an ally. However, the Filipino leaders also knew they needed the Chicanos and Mexicans if their strike was to be successful.

On September 16, Mexican Independence Day, hundreds of NFWA members jammed into the parish hall of Our Lady of

Guadalupe Church in Delano for the strike vote. Before the meeting ended, they had voted to demand the same wages as the Filipinos: $1.40 an hour and 25¢ for each box of grapes picked. Taking a cue from Mohandas K. Gandhi, the Indian independence leader, and from the African American struggle for freedom and justice, Chávez demanded that NFWA members take a vow to remain nonviolent. They shouted, "*Sí!*" Then the walls of the parish hall rocked with cries of *Huelga! Huelga! Huelga!*

STRIKE! STRIKE! STRIKE!

On September 20, 1965, four days after the historic vote, the NFWA walked out of the fields and went on strike with AWOC. Now more than thirty vineyards were affected. The NFWA, with more members than AWOC, shifted the balance of strikers from mostly Filipino to Chicano and Mexican.

The growers vowed to stand firm in their decision to keep wages the same and ignore the unions, no matter the consequences. Joseph G. Brosmer, managing director of the Agricultural Labor Bureau, representing growers in the area, said, "There is no interest on the part of the growers to carry on discussions of any kind with the union." Growers had become wealthy on cheap labor and federal subsidies that allowed them to purchase irrigation water for $123 per acre-foot, even though it cost the government $700 to deliver. They enjoyed federal guarantees against loss of certain crops. They saw no reason to change.

The California State Church Council, the main body of both Northern and Southern California Councils of Churches, sent a team of ministers to Delano to investigate the claims made by both striking workers and the growers. When Chávez refused earlier job offers from AWOC's Smith and the Peace Corps, many saw his actions as a voluntary vow of poverty. This and his belief in nonviolence made him popular among religious groups. The Reverend George Spindt, a member of the investigative team and pastor of the Messiah Lutheran Church in Redwood City, California, commented, "We were told [by growers] that the

"En nuestro rico Valle de San Joaquín, la mayor segmento de la sociedad está viviendo en la miseria."

....

"In our very rich San Joaquin Valley, the largest single segment of society is living in abject poverty."

unions have made no demands to the employers, so there is nothing yet to talk about, but letters sent to the growers by the unions have been returned unopened."

Not every farmer agreed with the thinking of agribusiness owners. Some who owned small, family-run farms and labored side by side with their hired seasonal help thought workers should get a better deal. Frederick Van Dyke of Stockton, California, supported the unionization of agricultural labor. In an open letter in 1959 to his fellow farmers, he listed several thoughts about how and why he'd arrived at this decision. The first was that as a church-going individual he could not "condone the fact that, in our very rich San Joaquin Valley, the largest single segment of society is living in abject poverty." He went on to suggest that "imported laborers take home to their native land approximately three-fourths of their net U.S. earnings. Business and the entire community would profit if this money were earned and spent" locally. Finally, he reasoned that if farmers paid higher wages, it would "benefit . . . agriculture itself" in the form of an increased, more reliable, and better trained labor supply. Van Dyke's view represented a small minority and was overshadowed by powerful and politically influential corporations or families that owned vast farms and saw profit, however gained, as their only obligation.

The plight of farm workers had been largely ignored by the American public after World War II. Then in November 1960, *CBS Reports* aired a documentary that focused a spotlight on what James P. Mitchell, U.S. secretary of labor under President Dwight D. Eisenhower, called "the excluded Americans." Reported by Edward R. Murrow, "Harvest of Shame" was shown the day after Thanksgiving to highlight the disparity between consumers, whose tables likely had been laden with food, and the farm laborers who had picked it. The prevailing attitude by growers toward those workers was best summed up by an anonymous farmer: "We used to own our slaves. Now we just rent them." The September 1965 AWOC strike unfolding in Delano, California, and supported by the NFWA brought the issue before the American public once again.

Many growers worried the strike would mean a ruined crop and lost profits. Others, especially the large, corporate-owned agribusinesses, predicted that workers would be staging a back-to-work movement within days. But workers did not march to regain their jobs. The vineyards in the Central Valley were too large and too spread out to picket all at once, even with more than two thousand workers now striking. So Itliong and Chávez agreed to a system of "roving picket lines needed to cope with a 'factory' of 400 square miles with over 10,000 'entrances'. They found the scabs and talked [many of] them out of the fields despite furious growers, hired gun-man 'guards', vicious dogs; police intimidation." These roving lines of strikers moved from one vineyard to another, from one farm entrance to the next. Only the picket captains and the striking workers themselves knew when and where they would take their positions. The picket captains were the strike leaders responsible for getting members to show up on time and at the right place and for making sure violence didn't break out on the protest lines.

From the strike's earliest days, Itliong had sent strikers not only to vineyard entrances and fields but also to the packing sheds and cold-storage plants, where grapes were processed and held for shipment. Chávez wanted to continue Itliong's approach. By picketing not only at the fields but also at the sheds and processing plants, he believed growers would become frustrated and angry to the point that they'd eventually make an embarrassing remark to reporters or do something they regretted. If this happened and the public learned the circumstances behind the strike, he felt certain donations would begin to pour in. He explained, "The best way [to do this] was to put them under pressure and let them express themselves to the public." Pressure, he believed, would be achieved by picketing at every imaginable location. It was a tactic he had learned from his days with Ross at the CSO and that Ross had learned by studying Alinsky: let the powerful show their true colors through their own words and actions. And the strike dragged on.

OPPOSITE: *From the very beginning of the strike, Itliong had encouraged his Filipino followers to picket on several fronts at once. Chávez borrowed the strategy from him and continued it as the strike wore on.*

Cada día, los dos huelgistas de los sindicatos se despertaron antes del alba para enfrentarse a algunas de las más grandes operaciones familiares o corporativas de cultivo.

....

Every day, the two unions' strikers rose before dawn to take on some of the biggest family and corporate farming operations.

Every day, the two unions' strikers rose before dawn to take on some of the biggest family and corporate farming operations in California, including Schenley Industries. Schenley owned the second-largest vineyard in the region and included among its brands Cutty Sark whiskey and Roma wine.

Most of the striking workers honored their pledge of nonviolence. But while Chávez was nonviolent, Itliong and many of the Filipino workers came from a background of militancy. Fights between growers, scabs, and strikers had broken out in the Coachella Valley vineyards before the strike there was settled in May. Through the Protestant California Migrant Ministry, with which Chávez had worked since his CSO days, he invited several prominent members of the clergy to help instill calm on the Schenley picket lines. The Migrant Ministry (which eventually became the National Farm Worker Ministry) was originally formed in 1920 in response to the extreme poverty of migrant farm workers in the southeastern United States. In the years that followed, it expanded to reach farming areas across the country. In addition to ministering to migrants' spiritual needs, it helped provide food, clothing, and health education and often acted as a contact between local schools and parents.

Just as the sun peeked over the mountains to the east, strikebreakers began arriving at the twenty entrances to the Schenley vineyards. From the sides of public roads, striking farm workers greeted them with calls to support their brothers and sisters of the fields. Some of the would-be scabs drove off, while others parked their vehicles and joined the picket lines. Those that reported to the fields didn't escape the farm workers' shouts. The strikers used bullhorns to broadcast their message into the affected vineyards.

Throughout the strike, the NFWA survived on donations of food and clothing from church and student groups and other liberal organizations interested in justice and fairness. AWOC shared its food with the NFWA at its kitchen in the Filipino Hall in Delano.

Huerta and Chávez (center)
meet with farm workers in an
unidentified field.

Pete Velasco, a longtime member of AWOC, was dedicated to unionizing farm workers. Because of his fund-raising skills, he was called Mr. Monies by union members.

During this time, Chávez continued to rise before dawn to make sure striking workers were in position and to caution them to remain nonviolent regardless of the actions of the other side. He believed that if the strikers turned to violence, the growers—who controlled the police and local judges—would crush the walkouts, and the strikers would surely lose in the court of public opinion. Itliong, along with AWOC's Velasco, and the NFWA's Huerta, Padilla, and Hernandez comprised a core leadership of picket captains who made daily rounds of the various picket locations. Padilla and Hernandez also continued to recruit new members across California. AWOC's Vera Cruz began to visit colleges and universities to speak to student groups, encouraging them to get involved in the farm-worker fight. Picket captains wrote reports of what happened on the picket lines, what was achieved, and the growers' reactions to the strike to share with the unions' membership. A report from Velasco dated December 6, 1965, demonstrated the strikers' dedication to la Causa: "An event that happened today confronts me with this question: 'When is a striker a real striker at heart?' The answer to this question is revealed in the following incident. On the 23rd of last month a . . . striker approached me and said, 'It is my last day today. I am going to Washington because my cousin is seriously ill. I will be back in about a week.' Today that brother is back to join us again."

Despite the two unions' welcoming attitude, some people thought labor strikes and negotiations were no places for women. Yet many of those forming the strike lines and carrying picket signs were women who worked in the fields side by side with the men. Huerta thought women on the picket line would help strikers remain peaceful. Despite this, she was encouraged by priests who supported the striking workers to go home and take care of her children, who often picketed with her. She soon won the priests' respect, however, by continuing to show up on the picket lines and refusing to back down when growers and their hired guards confronted her. Her tough, no-nonsense negotiating skills with growers and politicians in Sacramento made her a strong union ally. The priests who had questioned her abilities may have preferred that she stay home with her children, but they came to recognize that Huerta was an asset, as were the other women on the picket lines.

Soon, Chávez began traveling to colleges and universities to ask students for help. He urged them to give up their lunch money to help the strikers, passing around an empty box meant for packing grapes. He invited them to Delano to witness for themselves what farm workers were experiencing. Chávez wasn't a dynamic speaker or even a very good one, according to those who heard him. His message, though, was so heartfelt that many students, religious groups, and others journeyed to Delano. They were appalled when they saw the conditions under which

¿Cuando es un huelguista un huelguista de corazón?'

....

'When is a striker a real striker at heart?'

food was harvested for America's tables and the abuses strikers were enduring on the picket lines.

Chávez called on the Congress of Racial Equality (CORE) and the Student Nonviolent Coordinating Committee (SNCC) to join la Causa. Members of these two mixed-race student organizations had risked their lives to register voters in the South, sit in at segregated lunch counters, and ride buses during the Freedom Rides.

About a month into the strike, SNCC answered Chávez's call with offers of help. One of its volunteers was Marshall Ganz, a Harvard student who'd grown up in Bakersfield. He had been involved in the civil rights movement in the South and decided to see what was going on in Delano since it was so close to his boyhood home. It struck him that Delano "looked a lot . . . like Mississippi."

As articles began to appear in newspapers from Los Angeles to New York City, and as their harvests began to rot on the vines, growers realized this was no ordinary strike that they could easily dismiss. Rather than negotiate with farm workers, though, they sought court injunctions to limit peaceful picketing. They hired private security guards and thugs armed with shotguns and clubs to intimidate the strikers. They brought in strikebreakers from Los Angeles ghettos and from Mexico. But these replacement workers lacked experience, and so grape production yields declined.

As the strike continued, Velasco wrote, "The history of AWOC is never dull." Sometimes growers drove their trucks at dangerous speeds, "side-swiping the picket line with their cars and splashing muddy water on their [strikers'] faces" in an attempt to frighten picketers. The people dispersed to avoid being run down, but then regrouped, more determined than ever. One ranch foreman from the C. J. Lyons ranch grabbed a Huelga sign from one picket and blasted it with his shotgun. The foreman was the owner's son-in-law.

Other acts of intimidation occurred. Growers or their foremen would walk up to pickets and stomp on their toes or punch them in the ribs, often in full view of police officers, with no fear of retaliation—or arrest. Perhaps the most notorious act of violence during these first weeks of the strike occurred at a vineyard owned by two brothers, Bruno and Charles Dispoto. While shouting obscenities at the pickets, the brothers showered them with pesticides and threatened them with dogs. Although the Kern County prosecutor's office promised to investigate, no arrests were made. When Charles Dispoto beat up an AWOC volunteer, Governor Edmund G. "Pat" Brown's office finally demanded action.

Communists. Outside agitators. These were just some of the charges made against picketing strikers by Mothers Against Chávez and Citizens for Facts. These local groups were set up by growers and their families to counter-picket the strikers. The local growers, their families, and townspeople believed they had earned their way of life and refused to acknowledge that their treatment of workers was unfair or unjust. Yet one young woman's comment echoed the sentiment of most of her fellow farm workers: "I think they're used to treating the Mexican American and the Filipino like slaves. . . . They don't want to treat us like humans." One counter-protester who supported the

El capataz de algún rancho . . . le pegó un tiro con su escopeta a una pancarta de una demostración.

....

One ranch foreman . . . grabbed a Huelga sign from one picket and blasted it with his shotgun.

growers told a reporter, "We have no labor troubles [here]." The only problem she saw were the outsiders who were stirring up trouble with "our . . . workers." Local newspaper editorials painted the growers as victims of the strike action, despite their legal teams, political connections, and wealth.

The growers and their supporters attempted to undermine AWOC and the NFWA with every means available, and those were considerable. On October 6 the Federal Bureau of Investigation (FBI) received a phone call—the identity of the caller remains censored in FBI documents—that indicated "Chavez possibly has a subversive . . ." and "reportedly . . . a communist background." On October 7, another telephone contact reported that "several other individuals involved with the National Farm Workers Association . . . allegedly have subversive backgrounds. These individuals were identified as [the Reverend] Dave Havens, an organizer of the [National Farm Workers] Association and affiliated with the California Migrant Ministry; Larry Itliong and Ben Gines, organizers for the Agricultural Workers Organizing Committee; . . . and Delores [sic] Huerta, secretary of the National Farm Workers Association." Huerta, the informant claimed, was pictured in a "recent issue of 'The Worker' or some other communist publication" holding a sign that read "HUELGA." He further asserted that while the word means "strike," "Chavez told him it means more to the Mexican farm workers." The informant said that he'd been told that it meant "revolt." This was proven false when the FBI's own translator advised that "the word 'HUELGA' means 'strike' or to 'leave the place vacant'—to 'get out.'"

Although the FBI kept AWOC and the NFWA under surveillance, agents repeatedly concluded that the individuals named in the complaints had been involved in "no subversive activities." About Huerta, the bureau gave her a pass, pointing out that she had no "actual subversive activities . . . other than her association with CHAVEZ," who, the report determined, had "a 'clean' background."

Grower harassment didn't end there. Local judges issued more injunctions against assembling on the sides of public roads.

The Reverend Dave Havens attempted to read "Definition of a Strikebreaker," often attributed to American author Jack London, from a flatbed truck parked adjacent to a field where scabs had crossed the picket line. Sergeant Gerald Dodd of the sheriff's department ordered him to stop. London, author of *The Call of the Wild* and *White Fang*, among numerous other titles, referred to a strikebreaker as something made from the awful substance left over after God finished the rattlesnake, the toad, and the vampire. When Havens continued his reading anyway, Dodd ordered the preacher arrested for disturbing the peace and a squad car took him to the Kern County Jail.

El sheriff . . . prohibió el uso de la palabra huelga.

The sheriff . . . outlawed use of the word *huelga*.

Almost immediately, the sheriff then outlawed use of the word *huelga*. When protesters, including Chávez's wife, Helen, violated Dodd's order, forty-four people were arrested and taken to jail, including nine ministers. The Reverend Chris Hartmire of the California Migrant Ministry said the arrests helped rather than hurt the strike: "It makes the injustice so clear." But Loren Fote of the sheriff's department said shouting on the picket line "no longer serve[d] a worthwhile cause" because the strikebreakers already knew about the strike. Later, bail was set at $276 each, but Helen and a dozen other women remained in jail for three days. During this time, the NFWA prepared news releases about the incident and arrests for reporters covering the strike in the belief that newspaper accounts would further help sway public opinion.

The arrests of the forty-four certainly outraged college students caught up in the free-speech movement in Oakland and San Francisco. Students in those cities already were protesting

PRIVATE
PROPERTY
TRESPASSING
OR LOITERING
FORBIDDEN
BY LAW

Young people picked up strike flags. Many of them were on breaks from college, where they'd been active in the free-speech movement.

restrictions that had been placed on their political speech while on campuses. Chávez had spoken to students there only hours after the strikers were taken into custody. Hearing about the arrests, these students reached into their pockets and donated. On the way back to Delano, a couple of volunteers in the backseat of the car began counting the money, which had been tossed into several paper bags. "Sixty-seven hundred dollars in one dollar bills," said Chávez. "Besides the money, we got a lot of press." Suddenly, more young volunteers arrived in Delano to defy the growers, and contributions from around the country began to pour into the cash-strapped NFWA.

The police were relentless in their support of the growers. Edgar J. Gallardo, one of those on a picket line, describes a typical encounter:

"As I was being dragged by this zealous public servant, I tried to gain my footing and I asked, 'What's happening? Am I underarrest [sic].['] Feeling that I was trying to gain my footing, this dear fellow rammed his fist into my lumbar spine and began to shake me. His only reply to my question was, 'Keep moving.'

"With his fist in my spine and me up on my toes, it is my honnest [sic] opinion that this protector of fair haired children was hell bent on doing physical injury to me."

An unnamed protester is arrested in Kern County, California, where law enforcement officers supported the growers.

EL TEATRO CAMPESINO (THE FARM WORKERS' THEATER)

Among the young students who flooded into Delano to help support the strike was Luis Valdez. A college graduate, Valdez was from a Mexican American farm-worker family that had relocated from Delano to San Jose when he was a teen. Studying drama at San Jose State College, he discovered he had a knack for theatrics and later joined the San Francisco Mime Troupe. It was in San Francisco that he first met Chávez, who was on a speaking tour to build support for the strike. Valdez was happy that somebody was working to improve the lives of Mexican American farm workers. He joined the picket lines and later approached Chávez with a proposition. He asked if he could establish a theater company in the agitprop tradition. Agitprop theater focuses on political issues with an aim toward agitation (action) and propaganda (persuasion). He envisioned farm workers themselves staging comedy skits (*actos*) that would boost the morale of strikers and help persuade scabs to join the strike. Chávez, always happy to have volunteers, told Valdez he was willing to try

anything, but also pointed out there was no money to support it.

El Teatro Campesino burst onto the strike scene in October 1965. Performing in union halls and on flatbed trucks, the makeshift company staged skits using strikers who liked to ham it up in front of audiences. Without much in the way of scenery or costumes, the actors relied on hand-printed signs to identify their characters. The short ten- to fifteen-minute skits drew from the actors' experiences in the fields and on picket lines. They depicted the grower as the well-fed boss in sunglasses (or sometimes sporting a pig mask to point out growers' greed); Don Sotaco (the brainchild of cartoonist Andy Zermeño

from the newspaper *El Malcriado*) as the hapless, everyman field laborer; and the grower's bodyguard as a cigar chomping rent-a-thug. The skits resonated with farm workers, encouraging them to lose their fear by laughing at their opponents. They also irritated those in power.

··

Don Sotaco and the United Farm Workers Organizing Committee cower when meeting "a grower" (sporting a pig mask) carrying a club. The brief actos, or comedy skits, angered growers and their hired guards and were used to convince scabs to leave the fields and join the strike.

La NFWA empezó a seguir las uvas recolectadas desde su almacenamiento en cámaras frigorífica a los muelles de carga en San Francisco y Los Ángeles.

The NFWA began following harvested grapes from the cold-storage plants to loading docks in San Francisco and Los Angeles.

The FBI worried that Delano was ready to erupt into another Birmingham, where African American students in that Alabama city marched in May 1963 to protest segregation and second-class treatment. When the fire and police departments responded with water cannons and police dogs and the children were jailed, America's image was tarnished in the eyes of the world. With police turning a blind eye to the violent actions by growers and the courts supporting them through illegal injunctions, Delano was ripe for the same kind of violence.

In October, the NFWA began following harvested grapes from the cold-storage plants to loading docks in San Francisco and Los Angeles. There, they set up picket lines that longshoremen, the dock workers who loaded and unloaded the trucks, refused to cross. It was common for members of one union to respect the strike lines of other unions, just as the NFWA had done for AWOC. This combined action often brought an affected company to the bargaining table sooner than a strike called by a single union. Trucking companies and growers complained to the AFL-CIO that the longshoremen were violating their own contract. Longshoremen belonged to an AFL-CIO–backed union, the International Longshore and Warehouse Union. Al Green had been appointed in 1962 by AFL-CIO president George Meany to head AWOC. Green threatened Chávez that the Filipino union would break ranks with the NFWA if Chávez didn't stop compromising other unions by urging members to break their own contracts. Chávez didn't care. He stood up to Green, saying, "Don't you ever threaten me. . . . You're not even big enough to begin to carry out your threats." The struck companies filed a lawsuit. But while the suit worked its way through the courts, grape shipments were stopped.

On December 16, the powerful president of the United Auto Workers (UAW), Walter Reuther, visited the AWOC-NFWA strike. Like AWOC, the UAW was an AFL-CIO–backed union. It and other related labor groups got involved in the farm workers' struggle because they were reminded of their own battles to win better wages and safer working conditions from powerful

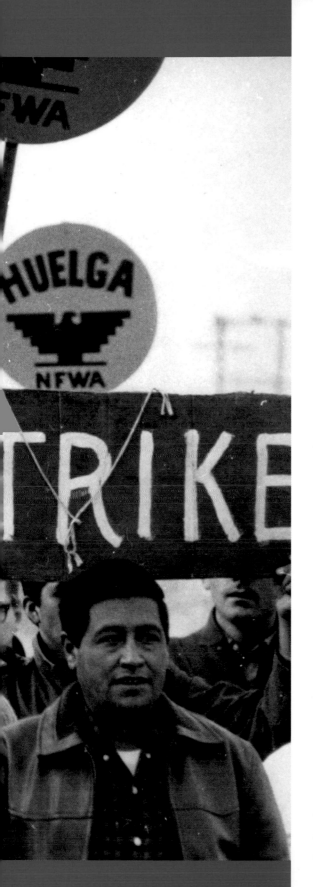

employers. They knew the only path to victory was for all unions to back each other. Bill Kircher, director of organizing for the AFL-CIO, explained, "I am sure that there were no more amateurish amateurs than those auto workers in Flint [Michigan] and the steel workers back in Gary [Indiana] and Youngstown [Ohio] who back in the mid-thirties decided that the time had come to have a union. . . . One of the benefits of the amateur organizer is that he doesn't know all the reasons . . . it can't be done."

In a meeting with Delano mayor Clifford Loader, Reuther warned, "The growers cannot win this dispute, and the sooner they realize this the less painful it will be."

Announcing that the UAW had pledged $5,000 a month to each of the two agricultural unions, Reuther marched with Itliong and Chávez down Delano streets carrying an NFWA picket sign and sang "We Shall Overcome." Only the day before, the police had warned that any protesters who marched in the city without a permit would be arrested. Having explained this new rule to Reuther, Chávez shared Reuther's response with a crowd of supporters: "Fine, let's go to jail together." When the chief of police arrived, ready to make arrests, he first noticed a crowd of reporters. Then he noticed Reuther and, according to Chávez, asked Reuther his name. When Reuther answered, the police chief did a double take. Then he said, "Well, I don't think I could arrest you." Arresting a Chicano field worker was one thing, but taking the Anglo head of the UAW into custody was something else entirely.

Itliong (left), Walter Reuther of the UAW (center), and Chávez (right) march in Delano the day after the chief of police said he would arrest any protesters parading without a permit.

Los pies

. . . .

Feet

Carrying the standard of Our Lady of Guadalupe, marchers set off to walk from Delano north to Sacramento. Chávez called it a peregrinación, *or pilgrimage, but not everyone was happy with the religious overtones of the march. Growers simply called it a publicity stunt.*

Prayer
of the Farm Workers Struggle

Show me the suffering of the most miserable;
So I will know my people's plight.

Free me to pray for others;
For you are present in every person.

Help me take responsibility for my own life;
So that I can be free at last.

Grant me courage to serve others;
For in service there is true life.

Give me honesty and patience;
So that I can work with other workers.

Bring forth song and celebration;
So that the Spirit will be alive among us.

Let the Spirit flourish and grow;
So that we will never tire of the struggle.

Let us remember those who have died for justice;
For they have given us life.

Help us love even those who hate us;
So we can change the world.

Amen.

AS THE STRIKE ENTERED THE NEW YEAR, BOTH SIDES DUG IN.

OPPOSITE: *César Chávez's "Prayer of the Farm Workers Struggle" asks for justice.*

Growers refused to negotiate or even recognize either union, and grape workers continued to hold out for their demands. On March 14, 1966, the U.S. Senate Subcommittee on Migratory Labor arrived in Delano to conduct hearings into who might be responsible for the misery and powerlessness of farm laborers in order to shape future protective legislation. They also wanted to investigate accusations of grower violence and police brutality on the picket lines. Among those on the panel were Senators George Murphy of California and, from New York, Robert F. Kennedy, brother of President John F. Kennedy, who had been assassinated in November 1963. President Kennedy, although he'd had no policy on agricultural workers, was popular with Chicanos because he was Catholic and had promised an end to racial discrimination. The president's popularity made Senator Robert Kennedy welcome among Chicano farm-worker communities. As Chávez recalled the day, "[Robert Kennedy] came and we picked him up at the airport. We took him, first, on a tour of the vineyards, and then took him to the picket lines. . . . I think he shook the hand of everyone in that picket line. . . . Then we took him to a little hall we had out there and . . . to the camp where we had our strike kitchen; then came back to the Filipino Hall [the striker's union hall] and [he] spoke briefly there. From there we went to the high school" where the hearing was held.

According to Chávez, "Senator Murphy was kind of put off because all the attention was given to Senator Kennedy when he came to the . . . farm worker. They'd . . . completely ignore him." Senator Murphy, a Republican, was a friend to California agribusiness, and farm workers viewed him with a wary eye.

In six months, the strike had grown from a simple walkout to a fledgling statewide and nationwide consumer boycott. In December, and with Huerta coordinating the action, the unions had taken the strike directly to consumers by asking them to stop buying California-grown grapes. With Schenley refusing to negotiate, the boycott was expanded to include this company's beverage brands. College students, through organizations like Students for a Democratic Society (SDS) and SNCC, offered to help with the boycott. Across the country, they passed out leaflets and picketed at markets that sold the company's brands of liquor and wine. (SDS began at the University of Michigan in Ann Arbor and spread to campuses across the country. A student-activist organization, it advocated individual power through participation in citizen lobbies and criticized racial discrimination, economic inequality, and big business. Practicing nonviolence, SDS was drawn to the grape pickers' strike, as was SNCC, despite SDS's nonunion stance.) AWOC and NFWA also sent small crews of migrants into urban areas where Schenley products were sold to picket, to recruit volunteers, and to coordinate local boycott efforts. For many of the farm workers, it was the first time they'd traveled beyond California's borders.

No one had ever used a boycott of products in a labor dispute before. Chávez borrowed the idea from Mohandas Gandhi's twenty-four day, 240-mile march in 1930 to India's seaside to collect salt himself rather than pay the British tax on it if he purchased it. It was an act of civil disobedience, and it drew worldwide attention when Gandhi was arrested. This simple act helped change Great Britain's attitudes toward granting India its independence. Chávez was also familiar with the thirteen-month-long bus boycott in Montgomery, Alabama, which was sparked by the December 1955 arrest of Rosa Parks. Parks, an African American woman, had refused to give up her bus seat to a white man. In the months that followed her conviction, African Americans in that city walked or shared rides with those who had cars to protest laws that required them to sit in the back of buses. Now explaining the Schenley boycott, Chávez said, "The consumer boycott is the only open door in the dark corridor of nothingness down which farm workers have had to walk for so many years. It is a gate of hope through which they expect to find the sunlight of a better life for themselves and their families."

As picketing continued through winter's chill, leaders talked about a march to place the farm workers' grievances before Governor Brown and the state legislature. The march, called a *peregrinación* ("pilgrimage"), had strong roots in the Catholic faith and began on Thursday, March 17, 1966, just twelve hours after the Senate subcommittee finished its hearings. Some two hundred people, including children, set off to march from NFWA headquarters in Delano to Sacramento, some three hundred miles to the north. It was a "pilgrimage of a cultural minority who have suffered from a hostile environment and who now mean business," Chávez explained. "It is a fight for bread and dignity."

Leading the march, along with Chávez and Itliong, were Jack Conway, head of the seven-million-member AFL-CIO Industrial Union Department, and Paul Schrade, regional director of the United Auto Workers. Joining them were marchers carrying the standard of Our Lady of Guadalupe, the patron saint of Mexico and the workers' symbol of hope. Others carried the flags of Mexico, the Philippines, and the United States, as well as the banners of the NFWA and AWOC. One marcher shouldered a large wooden cross. Chávez was criticized by some in both unions for turning the march into a religious pilgrimage, but it was what he wanted.

The march had barely begun, however, when it ran into an obstacle. Because the marchers didn't have a parade permit, Delano police chief James Ailes ordered a blockade on the road leading to the downtown business district. (In many communities, a permit was required before any large assembly of people could stage a march.) Twenty police officers blocked their way. When the marchers refused to travel on roads that skirted around the town, Ailes and the city manager agreed to issue a permit rather

"Es una lucha por el pan y la dignidad."

. . . .

"It is a fight for bread and dignity."

than play into the hands of the unions. The pilgrimage was being covered by the national media, which had been drawn to Delano by Senator Kennedy and the Senate subcommittee hearings. While permit details were being worked out, clergymen led the marchers in prayers and songs.

Al Green of AWOC had not wanted his group to march because he thought of it as a civil rights protest rather than a tactic used by legitimate labor unions (and because of his earlier disagreement with Chávez). But Itliong overruled him, as did Bill Kircher, Green's boss. In addition, Kircher ordered Green to prepare a huge AFL-CIO welcome for the marchers when they arrived in Modesto. Kircher wanted to show the country that the large affiliation of unions was united behind the farm workers.

The pilgrimage zigzagged north through small farm communities, where each evening marchers held a rally with local field laborers and supporters. They depended on the charity of farm workers and supportive townspeople along the way for food and shelter. Remaining in Delano after walking a short distance, Itliong and Huerta kept up pressure on Schenley and the other growers through daily strike lines. Few people made every step of the pilgrimage from Delano to Sacramento. They would drop out and then drop in again at another location, but each day, the number of pilgrims grew.

The growers continued to say the strike had not hurt the grape harvest and dismissed the march as a publicity stunt. But grape shipments told a different story. Longshoremen at West Coast ports still refused to handle struck grapes, leaving trucks full of the fruit on the docks. Trucking companies and growers filed suit against the longshoremen. When the decision came down, it declared the longshoremen couldn't refuse to handle the Delano grapes. Despite this, the International Longshore and Warehouse Union said it would ignore the ruling for the time being. Eventually, according to an undated *Delano Grapevine* article, grape shipments at Giumarra Vineyards Corporation—known as the "'Table Grape King'"—dropped "by more than 75%." The strike was beginning to affect the growers' incomes.

Gilbert Padilla, an NFWA vice president and, later, a UFW assistant director (circa 1960s)

In response to growers' claims that the pilgrimage was a publicity stunt, Chávez told a *Los Angeles Times* reporter that "the theme of the march is 'pilgrimage . . . and revolution.'" He went on to explain that it was "also a march of penance—public penance for the sins of the strikers, their own personal sins and perhaps their yielding to feelings of hatred and revenge." Despite these comments, Chávez was smart enough to realize that a little theatricality was good for attracting people to his cause. Sometimes with Itliong at his side, images of Chávez limping on blistered feet appeared on evening news broadcasts throughout the state and the country. For many, the peregrinación was the defining moment of the Delano grape strike.

Shortly before the workers arrived in Sacramento, Gilbert Padilla told Chávez that Schenley Industries wanted a meeting with the NFWA. At first, Chávez thought it was a hoax, but when it turned out to be real, the Reverend Chris Hartmire drove Chávez and a few others to the Beverly Hills mansion of Schenley's lawyer. Besides Chávez and Schenley's lawyer, the AFL-CIO's Kircher and a representative from the Teamsters were there. As Chávez recalled, Kircher refused to be in the same room with anybody from the Teamsters. Chávez became angry when they couldn't decide who was going to negotiate on behalf of the farm workers. Finally, Chávez threatened to leave, saying, "Talk to me about my Union, not to the AFL-CIO or the Teamsters." His outburst suggested that he may have forgotten his Filipino strike brothers.

A preliminary union contract was negotiated with Chávez. He was weary but happy that the strike and boycott seemed to be working. Helping to bring Schenley to the bargaining table were reports that bartenders were considering a boycott of the company's liquors in sympathy with the strikers. Also, the NFWA, with the help of the Teamsters, who refused to cross the union's picket lines, had basically shut down the company's San Francisco warehouse. Speaking about Schenley's change of heart on April 6, Kircher declared, "Labor history was written here today." That very same day, though, "the Council of California Growers released a statement saying that Schenley was 'not representative

"*Los trabajadores agrícolas . . . tenemos que competir también— por el nivel de vida, para dar a nuestras familias su pan de cada día.*"

"The farm workers . . . must also compete—with the standard of living to give our families their daily bread."

NFWA members and their children at an evening union meeting at Eagles Hall in Porterville, California, 1966

of California agriculture where growers steadfastly refuse to sell out their employes [*sic*] and force them into a union that does not represent them.'"

Seven months after the Filipino and Chicano strikers left the vineyards and twenty-five days after marchers left Delano, some eight thousand to ten thousand ecstatic pilgrims and their supporters jammed the west plaza of the state capitol grounds in Sacramento. It was April 10, Easter, and the skies turned from sunny to rainy and back again. The unions demanded that Governor Brown meet with them, but he had left for a Palm Springs vacation a few days earlier. Encouraged by the Schenley development, Huerta told the crowd, "We are no longer interested in . . . the excuses the Governor has to give in defense of the growers . . . or why the growers cannot dignify the workers as individuals with the right to place the price on their own labor through collective bargaining [union negotiating].

"The Governor maintains that the growers are in a competitive situation. Well, the farm workers are also. We must also compete—with the standard of living to give our families their daily bread."

The Schenley agreement to recognize the NFWA was the first major break for Chávez's union, but Kircher noted it was the AFL-CIO and AWOC that had brought Schenley and the NFWA together. He added, "We look forward to the day when this movement is part of the great mainstream of organized labor, the AFL-CIO." When asked if the NFWA planned to join the AFL-CIO, Chávez sidestepped the question, saying only, "We realize that we are now entering the big leagues and we will soon be part of the mainstream of the labor movement." Some of AWOC's Filipinos who had been wary of the NFWA as a competitor now had cause for worry.

The Schenley agreement sent shock waves through the remaining California growers. Workers now were fired simply for taking leaflets from strikers. Guards patrolled the vineyards to keep strikers and organizers out. Those organizers who managed to get into the fields were often met by violence or arrested for trespassing. And if foremen saw union organizers talking with workers in the fields, the workers were fired on the spot. At one point, however, Huerta sent her nine-year-old son, Emilio, into the Di Giorgio ranch with a handful of flyers to give to scab workers. Di Giorgio was a huge agribusiness enterprise known for its underhanded tactics and for violence against pickets. Huerta chose Emilio for the same reason she'd lobbied for women on the picket lines; she reasoned women and children were less likely to become victims of violence. Some moments after going in, Emilio came running back out "as fast as his little legs would carry him," chased by Di Giorgio's personnel manager in a car. Fortunately, the child wasn't hurt. He had also managed to get the flyers to the scabs.

The Schenley victory was sweet, but short-lived. Pickets were removed from Schenley's vineyards and the boycott against the company's products was ended. Nevertheless, Chávez vowed to continue to apply pressure to the dozens of other grape growers refusing to recognize the union.

All but forgotten now was AWOC, as the strike coverage in newspapers and on television became more about Chávez and his union, the NFWA.

Three days after the march ended, the NFWA started all-out picketing at Di Giorgio Fruit Corporation. On April 6, Robert Di Giorgio, president of the company, wrote to AWOC's Itliong to propose secret-ballot elections at its four California farms to determine if workers wanted a union to represent them: "Di Giorgio Corporation urges that the California State Conciliation Service conduct immediate secret-ballot elections on its Di Giorgio Farms, Sierra Vista Ranch, and at its Dantoni and New England Orchards to determine if its employees wish to be represented . . . by any labor union." Although the NFWA now was the dominant union in the news, AWOC was still working with it toward their common goal. In an April 8 telegram to Di Giorgio, the governor urged "all parties to cooperate in working out mutually acceptable answers to such questions as [they] develop the terms of the consent agreement." Governor Brown even offered the "good offices of my

AWOC estaba casi olvidado por completo ahora.

....

All but forgotten now was AWOC.

Don Coyote, the growers' contractor, threatens Don Sotaco, who represents the poor, often naive worker. In this scene, however, Don Sotaco seems to know exactly what is going on. Whose side will he be on?

administration" as the parties worked out a procedure to solve "the mutually unsatisfactory economic and social unrest which has persisted in the Delano area." Chávez said that after the march, "The boycott . . . began to pick up speed right away. There were a lot of people who had fought DiGiorgio [*sic*] in the thirties and the forties and the fifties who started coming out of the woodwork to take them on in Chicago, San Francisco, New York." He ordered boycott groups across the country to remain on alert in case the company didn't live up to the Schenley example.

Las tortugas

....

Turtles

While growers got local courts to issue orders that prohibited picketing along the roadsides at ranch entrances, the orders didn't forbid praying. Moving from one entrance to the next, this portable altar built on the back of Chávez's station wagon allowed union members to spread their message while they remained within the law.

Dolores Huerta on a picket line in an undated photo

Di Giorgio
guards threatened
a female union
organizer with
a gun and
knocked her to
the ground.

ALMOST AS SOON AS THE SCHENLEY AGREEMENT WAS REACHED,

an AFL-CIO representative from Los Angeles suggested to Chávez that the NFWA's twenty-five hundred members merge with AWOC and become one powerful union under the AWOC banner. Chávez refused the idea of a merger, saying his Chicano strikers had fought too hard and bled too much to give it all away. Bill Kircher agreed with Chávez's decision but gently kept suggesting a merger.

Encouraged by the Schenley victory, Chávez sat down with Di Giorgio representatives in Fresno to iron out details to the secret-ballot election as mentioned in the company's April 6 letter to Itliong. However, negotiations broke down almost immediately when Di Giorgio guards threatened a female union organizer with a gun and knocked her to the ground. They struck her fellow worker with such force that he needed thirteen stitches to close the wound.

The Di Giorgio Fruit Corporation was fiercely antiunion and had a reputation for keeping union representatives out of its fields. In 1939, the company had defeated strikers in Yuba City, California, with the help of a sheriff's gang that beat protesters and drove them out of town. In 1948, it illegally brought in bracero workers to break a strike. When the braceros stopped work and joined the strikers in sympathy, Di Giorgio turned to a political ally. Richard M. Nixon, then a Republican congressman from California, launched an investigation and suggested the strike was a Communist plot.

Chávez knew the NFWA was facing a giant in agriculture that was comfortable doing whatever it needed to do to prevent the unionization of its workers. The union leader planned to hit

Algunos volvieron a cruzar los piquetes para trabajar. Entonces Chávez añadió otra táctica . . . una desaceleración del trabajo, o planes de tortuga.

. . . .

Some drifted back across the picket line for work. This was when Chávez added another tactic . . . a work slowdown, or *planes de tortuga.*

Di Giorgio both in the fields and also in the cities where the company's products were sold. He turned to the weapon that had proved most successful against Schenley. Three days after the march ended, he called for a boycott against Di Giorgio products. These included its TreeSweet brand of canned, frozen, and bottled fruit juices as well as canned foods—tomatoes, beans, peaches, apricots, and corn, among other products— carrying the S&W Fine Foods label.

Workers were simultaneously on strike at vineyards and ranches all over the valley, but many were weary and could no longer get by on the meager support the NFWA offered. At Di Giorgio, some drifted back across the picket line for work. This was when Chávez added another tactic to those already in place: a work slowdown, or *planes de tortuga* ("turtle plans"), within the ranch. Some of the strikers who crossed the picket line for employment had secretly agreed to work at a turtle's pace. This allowed them to earn some income while costing Di Giorgio money in terms of slowed production. They also agreed to relay company plans and strategies to the NFWA, but as Di Giorgio workers, they would be able to cast votes in a ranch election to determine if they wanted any union representation at all, as called for in the April 6 letter to Itliong.

At the same time, Di Giorgio was forcing workers to sign cards authorizing the Teamsters to be their union representatives, an alarming development. The Teamsters had been expelled from the AFL-CIO in 1957 for corruption and its connection to mobsters, organized crime, and violence against those that opposed them. The AFL-CIO, fearing the federal government would pass legislation limiting union activities, ended its backing of the organization. Ever since, strong tensions remained between the two groups. Mostly representing the trucking and construction industries, the Teamsters had largely ignored field laborers. It had only one contract covering farm workers in Salinas Valley, and it favored the grower. Now, the union allowed itself to be used by Di Giorgio to try to nudge the NFWA and AWOC out of the picture.

Following the Call to boycott Di Giorgio brands, the director of personnel for Di Giorgio sent a June 4 letter to all employees of the company's Sierra Vista ranch in Delano. In it, he said, "Mr. Ceasar [sic] Mosquito is buzzing around and like all mosquitos, he does nothing more than buzz and make a pest of himself." He added that the Schenley agreement was not in the workers' best interests because Schenley would likely "raise no more table grapes" and this would mean that "many jobs will disappear."

In May 1967, a judge friendly to the company issued an injunction limiting the number of people who could picket its Sierra Vista ranch in Delano. The union's hands were tied, but three women approached Chávez with an idea. The injunction limited picketing. But did it limit praying across from the ranch entrance? Knowing that most of the strikers were Catholic, Chávez thought it was a great idea. He enlisted Richard's help to build a portable altar that would sit on the back of Chávez's old station wagon.

The next morning, the NFWA announced it would not picket Di Giorgio's Sierra Vista ranch but instead would hold a prayer meeting. Local Spanish-language radio stations also made the announcement. That morning, the strikers flocked to pray at the shrine on the back of the station wagon across from the main entrance of the ranch. Adorned with flowers, flickering candles, and images of Our Lady of Guadalupe, the mobile shrine attracted strikebreakers as well as strikers. Stopping to pray, the scabs were embraced by the strikers, received a little religion, and heard why the strike had been called against Di Giorgio. Many returned to the fields, but many others joined the strikers—or left the area altogether. Indeed, so many Di Giorgio strikebreakers came out of their houses on the ranch to pray at the makeshift altar that the ranch's armed guards couldn't figure out who were employees and who were strikers. Strikers took advantage of the guards' confusion to go into the vineyards and pass out union leaflets right under their noses.

While the strike against Di Giorgio turned into a prayer vigil, little bands of AWOC and NFWA volunteers fanned out

Fueron retenidos durante horas bajo el sol abrasador del desierto.

....

They were held for hours under the blazing desert sun.

across the United States and into Canada. San Francisco. Chicago. New York City. Toronto. Toledo. Boston. Baltimore. Philadelphia. Washington, D.C. In each city, these volunteers carried picket signs asking consumers to boycott Di Giorgio's products. They spoke with consumers about what it was like to be an American field worker. They urged grocery stores and supermarkets to remove the company's products from their shelves.

On a financial level, the boycott against Di Giorgio didn't strike the blow that Chávez had hoped. Di Giorgio was a major corporation with many sources of income. Agricultural products made up only a small portion. Even so, it hurt the company in other ways. Di Giorgio's often violent responses to the strikers and boycotters, including the use of hired thugs who carried weapons, created a disturbing public image, especially when captured by television news crews or newspaper photographers.

Chávez and Kircher sat down with company officials again, this time at its San Francisco headquarters, for another round of negotiations. The pair learned that Di Giorgio had scheduled an election at its Delano and Borrego Springs ranches. The ballots already were printed offering workers four choices: the Teamsters union, the NFWA, AWOC, and no union. Although Chávez and the NFWA now had more of the media's attention than did AWOC, Di Giorgio hoped to divide the votes between the two unions to increase the Teamsters' chances of winning.

Caught off guard by the surprise development, Chávez made a quick trip to Borrego Springs, in the desert area of eastern San Diego County, to campaign among Di Giorgio workers for the NFWA. When the results were announced, the election went to the Teamsters. It won by offering workers bribes of beer and by telling them Chávez was a Communist.

Even though it lost the election, the NFWA had supporters at the Borrego Springs ranch. Before the election, a couple of workers had left the fields to join the NFWA picket line, leaving their belongings behind in the company's housing. After the Teamster victory, Chávez knew the men would be unable to return to work. He offered to help them get their belongings.

Accompanying Chávez and the two workers were Reverend Hartmire and Father Victor Salindini, a Catholic priest and union supporter. Just as they entered the ranch, they were met by armed security guards who forced Chávez, Hartmire, and Salindini into an enclosed truck, where they were held for hours under the blazing desert sun. Later that night, sheriff's deputies shackled the three men together and took them to the county jail in San Diego, where they were strip-searched and held overnight.

Di Giorgio's tactics backfired. When workers learned how Chávez and the two clergymen were treated, many more abandoned the Borrego Springs ranch and joined la Causa. The NFWA challenged the election as unlawful, and two weeks

Police arrest a peaceful protester after she was beaten by thugs hired by growers.

after the arrests, Governor Brown ordered Di Giorgio to hold a new election. By then, Chávez realized the importance of the rescheduled Di Giorgio vote. The NFWA could remain an independent union and threaten the outcome of future elections, as it had in Borrego Springs. Or it could merge with AWOC as the AFL-CIO had earlier suggested. He understood there was strength in numbers and in a united front, the philosophy behind unionization. He agreed to a merger vote. In August 1966, the NFWA and AWOC became one, now calling itself the United Farm Workers Organizing Committee (UFW). Chávez was selected by the merged unions' executive board of Chicano and Filipino leaders to be its director, and Itliong was named assistant director. However, distrust between the two groups still remained. Filipino Ben Gines, who had helped negotiate the May 1965 wage increases in the Coachella Valley and stood with Itliong when workers walked out of the Delano vineyards in September, left the union and joined the Teamsters. When the new Di Giorgio election was held on August 30, the UFW was victorious—but not before Di Giorgio hurled another salvo by laying off two hundred UFW supporters just days ahead of the election.

The high profile of the peregrinación and the Schenley victory inspired farm workers across the country to protest for better wages and living conditions. In the southern part of Texas in the Rio Grande Valley, four hundred melon pickers, mostly Chicano, shook up growers and state politicians by staging a June 1966 strike against La Casita Farms. They had been talking about a strike for years but were energized by the successes in Delano. The workers asked Eugene Nelson, an organizer in the Delano grape strike, to relocate to Mission, one of the towns in the valley, and together, they formed the Independent Workers Association (IWA). Robin Lloyd, a reporter for the *Washington Post*, explained, "They feel that the 45 cents an hour . . . for field work isn't enough." The field laborers were asking for $1.25 per hour. Wages in the Rio Grande Valley ranged from 45¢ to a high of 85¢ an hour, while growers made a profit of $500 per acre. The IWA chose two mottos: "now is the time" and "all we want is justice."

"Solo queremos justicia."

....

"All we want is justice."

On the first day of the strike, 80 percent of the work force stayed off the job, and the growers began bringing in strikebreakers from Mexico. Despite the mass walkout, picketing was weak, partially because of a local ordinance brought about by growers "that require[d] pickets be at least 50 feet apart."

Although the protests were peaceful, local law enforcement asked for assistance from the Texas Rangers, which were formed in 1823 to help protect frontier settlers from Indian raids, outlaws, and Mexican bandits. In 1935, the Rangers were placed under the Texas Department of Public Safety and were given the same power as sheriffs. The IWA, the priests and Protestant clergy supporting the strikers, and the AFL-CIO accused the Rangers of illegal arrests, beating strikers, and using unnecessary force. The AFL-CIO's Kircher said, "The Rangers have come in and placed themselves squarely on the side of the employers." Ralph Yarborough, U.S. senator from Texas, denounced the law enforcement agency as "hired strikebreakers." In one month, some sixty-five strikers were arrested. The strike drew national attention after one UFW organizer, Magdaleno Dimas, suffered a split scalp inflicted, he said, by a shotgun wielded by Ranger captain A. Y. Allee. Allee denied the charge. "Hell," he said, "I wouldn't hurt a dog if he wasn't biting me." He went on to say, "Those people . . . started to picket 15 or 20 at a time; they didn't work and didn't want to. They said they wanted to be arrested, by George, and I accommodated them."

With growers refusing to acknowledge the IWA or even to consider the workers' demands, Nelson decided to take their grievances directly to Texas governor John Connally in Austin, the state capital. Beginning July 4, 1966, a small band of striking workers set off on the two-month-long, four-hundred-mile trek from southern Texas north to Austin. The marchers, around three hundred, carried red Huelga flags. The UFW black eagle was also present. Now and then, they would break into a song written for the occasion, the last line of which said, in English, "If there is no satisfaction in Austin, then it is on to Washington." Only about twenty-five marchers made every step of the journey, but one

En las primeras veinticuatro horas desde su llegada, la pareja fue detenida por una alteración del orden público, por liderar un grupo de simpatizantes en la Oración del Señor.

....

Within twenty-four hours of their arrival, the pair was arrested for disturbing the peace while leading a group of supporters in the Lord's Prayer.

stood out—"a gray burro with $1.25 painted in pink on his side." Chávez joined the marchers for a short distance before hurrying off to a reception held in his honor.

The governor, meeting them before they arrived in Austin, said he "sympathized with the workers," but he refused to do anything about their situation. Father Sherrill Smith, a Catholic priest who had walked most of the way, called the governor's visit "a slap in the face, a pat on the head, the great white father type of thing." In Austin, some six thousand to ten thousand people turned out to support the Rio Grande Valley strikers at a rally the next day.

With no resolution to the Texas strike in sight, Chávez sent Gilbert Padilla, one of the vice presidents of the UFW, to Texas to help out. Padilla was joined by the Reverend Jim Drake. While Itliong and Dolores Huerta remained in Delano to coordinate and supervise the ongoing strike and boycott against Di Giorgio, Chávez called for a boycott against La Casita Farms.

Since the Texas Rangers were still harassing and jailing striking farm workers in the Rio Grande Valley, Chávez suggested to Padilla that he and Drake teach the Rangers the power of prayer. Within twenty-four hours of their arrival, the pair was arrested for disturbing the peace while leading a group of supporters in the Lord's Prayer. According to the complaint, the janitor who was cleaning the courthouse said "that he was prevented [by the demonstrators] from performing his job properly." But he was working on the third floor of the building at least sixty feet away from Drake's little group.

Released from jail the next day, the pair quickly organized women family members of "Magdaleno Dimas—his grandmother, his mother, his sisters—dressed in black [to pray] for the Rangers' souls" outside the hotel where the Rangers met every afternoon. The scene was covered by the press and so embarrassed politicians in Austin, including Governor Connally, that the Texas Rangers left town.

The drive to unionize workers in Texas was also joined by a young attorney who was convinced by Chávez to team up with

the UFW. Jerry Cohen, a recent law-school graduate from the University of California at Berkeley, "was attracted by the UFW's marches up and down the San Joaquin [Central] Valley." He had also joined picket lines at his local market to protest its sale of Perelli-Minetti wines. The union was boycotting Perelli-Minetti because it had signed a grower-friendly contract with the Teamsters. When Cohen met Chávez, he was unaware that the union leader already knew about his protests through contacts on the picket line. And when Chávez invited him to join the union struggle as its general counsel, Cohen was forced to admit that as a new lawyer he didn't know much. "[Chávez] lied," said Cohen, "and said he didn't know anything either and that we would learn it together."

Cohen became the union's first general counsel in 1967 and soon found himself in Texas where he borrowed a tactic commonly used in the South by African Americans fighting for their civil rights: get arrested for disobeying unconstitutional laws and fight the legality of those arrests in court. Cohen realized it was no different in farm areas where the economy relied on growers. Local and state courts often bent to the growers' will, slapping injunctions on pickets that would limit the strikers' ability to peacefully assemble or even the speech they were allowed to use. When strikers were arrested for violating these illegal laws, Cohen would appeal their cases to higher courts and before judges who were fairer. The appeals also brought increased media attention to the injustices farm workers faced. Most of the injunctions placed against the union eventually would be overturned as unconstitutional, but by that time the strikes would be over.

Jerry Cohen, the UFW's legal counsel, testifies before a U.S. Senate hearing (date unknown).

Huelga de hambre

....

Hunger Strike

Andy Imutan, Dolores Huerta, Larry Itliong, and Robert F. Kennedy (from left to right) at the Mass celebrating the end of Chávez's twenty-five-day fast

Children, often as young as six years of age, were sometimes used as strikebreakers, working side by side with their parents.

IN DELANO, THE GRAPE STRIKE CONTINUED AT VINEYARDS BIG AND SMALL.

Some growers now voluntarily raised wages, but others continued to hire children as young as six years of age to work in the fields as scabs. During the summer of 1967, the UFW picked its next big target, the family-run Giumarra Vineyards Corporation, located near Bakersfield. The corporation farmed more than eleven thousand acres in the Central Valley. Meanwhile, the UFW began reaching agreements on union contracts with major California wineries, including Gallo, Christian Brothers, and Paul Masson, in other parts of the state.

On August 3, 1967, workers voted to strike Giumarra. Two-thirds of Giumarra's work force of around five thousand farm laborers walked out of the vineyards, leaving grapes that were ready to be harvested hanging on the vines. Immediately, Giumarra brought in strikebreakers. The company obtained court injunctions against UFW that prohibited the use of bullhorns on picket lines, limited the number of demonstrators at each entrance to the vineyard to three, and required each picket to stand at least three hundred feet apart. While Jerry Cohen, now the UFW's full-time attorney, sought relief through the courts, Chávez called for a nationwide boycott of the company's grapes.

The union obtained agreements from more than three hundred independent markets to discontinue sale of Giumarra grapes. It also won agreements from several chain stores. Giumarra, however, was a step ahead of the union and ready for this boycott action. It began shipping grapes under the labels of thirty other California and Arizona table-grape growers. Huerta and Ross urged Chávez to call for a boycott of *all* California table grapes. By January 1968, with Giumarra continuing to mislabel its grapes, Chávez gave in to their advice. He also wrote to John Gardner, U.S. secretary of health, education, and welfare, explaining the situation: "This is to verify our conversation by phone Thursday afternoon in which I outlined to you our problem with the Giumarra Vineyards Corporation. We have been on strike against Giumarra since August 3rd, 1967. During the harvest, the Giumarra Vineyards Corporation used

Giumarra estaba un paso por delante del sindicato . . . y de la acción del boicot. Empezó a comercializar sus uvas bajo las marcas de otros treinta productores de uvas de mesa de California y Arizona.

Giumarra was a step ahead of the union and . . . boycott action. It began shipping grapes under the labels of thirty other California and Arizona table-grape growers.

other growers' labels to ship its grapes in an effort to avoid our nationwide boycott of his product.

"We referred this matter in complaint to the Regional Office in San Francisco of the Pure Food and Drug Administration. They investigated the matter and returned a verdict to us stating that this was in specific violation of the law."

Andy Imutan led the boycott in Baltimore and most major East Coast cities, and he found a unique way to strike back at Giumarra through one-to-one negotiation. He approached produce managers at each Baltimore market not already cooperating with the boycott and asked them to order one less box of California grapes each week. They agreed. It was a successful strategy because it meant fewer and fewer grapes were ordered and the produce managers still were able to keep their jobs while supporting the boycott.

Giumarra was the largest fresh table-grape grower in the country, with sales of at least $12 million per year. Additionally, it received one-sixth of the proceeds from numerous oil wells on its property, and in 1967 the company collected a government subsidy of almost a quarter of a million dollars for not planting cotton. Government subsidies were payments by the federal government to farmers. Beginning during the Great Depression when farms were mostly small, family-run operations, they were meant to make sure farmers had money to live on and continue farming, while also keeping food prices low enough for the average American to afford. To do this, the government sometimes paid farmers, as in Giumarra's case, not to plant a crop in order to maintain its price or to conserve soil. An agreement similar to the one the UFW reached with Schenley Industries would have cost Giumarra around $625,000 a year, just a little more than twice its government subsidy.

As the national boycott of all grapes and the battle against Giumarra unfolded, some union members were getting impatient. They began threatening to respond to growers' violence with violence of their own. On the Giumarra strike lines, hired guards made a show of their weapons and shoved and struck protesters. They spat in strikers' faces, taunting them. Local police arrested the protesters for standing too close together or for causing the disturbance. Some strikers spoke of setting fire to growers' sheds or vandalizing their equipment. Others talked of burning crops. Still others accused Chávez of cowardice for refusing to give blow for blow. A few even said they were going to arm themselves.

The grape strike was just one episode of several that were shaking the United States to its core. The controversial war in Vietnam was claiming thousands of lives, and young antiwar protesters on college campuses and in city streets were being met by angry police officers, beatings, and tear gas. Widespread

Children joined the picket lines right beside their parents when a boycott of all grapes was called.

civil rights demonstrations were spreading in cities as African Americans demanded equality that had been denied them. Evening news broadcasts were filled with images of an America at war with itself. Now, on the strike lines, some agricultural workers were talking about taking revenge.

In February 1968, Chávez feared his own people might seek "a short-cut to victory." Something had to be done to prevent the farm-worker movement from turning violent. Once again, he took his cue from Gandhi, who had fasted to preserve his own followers' nonviolence during their decades-long struggle to win India's independence from Britain.

Chávez, now forty, began his fast, or hunger strike, on February 15, quietly and without fanfare. A few days later, he told a meeting of strikers at the Filipino Hall about the fast and why he had stopped eating. He told followers, "We cannot build a strong union and bring dignity to farm workers based on violence." Recalling the lessons his mother taught him as a child about using his brain and tongue to avoid trouble, he believed peaceful protest was critical to the movement's success. "The deliberate taking of the life of a grower would make the cause for which we fight meaningless."

Then he walked several miles to the Forty Acres, a parcel of land west of Delano purchased in 1966 that was headquarters for the farm-worker movement. There, he moved into a small, almost monastic room with a single bed at the union's service station. The room originally had been intended for storage. Helen thought he was being ridiculous. She walked part of the way with him, arguing the whole time to talk him out of fasting. But Chávez was stubborn, and she eventually gave up.

Every day, hundreds of supporters camped out and gathered at the Forty Acres to celebrate a Catholic Mass. They prayed for Chávez and the union's goals. They prayed that peace would return to the valley. Chávez vowed to continue the fast until all the strikers rededicated themselves "to our commitment to nonviolence as a means of achieving our goal, which is the dignity of farm workers."

Chávez terminó el ayuno cuando "el senador buscó un pedazo de pan y me lo dio."

Chávez ended the fast when "the Senator got a piece of bread and gave it to me."

Growers watched in disbelief. The national news media flocked to the Forty Acres to report on the event. The fast restored the farm workers' hope and resolve to remain nonviolent, while it elevated Chávez to an almost martyr-like station among poor Chicano farm workers. But once again, a few critics complained, uncomfortable with Chávez's religious imagery.

On the thirteenth day of the fast, a noticeably weakened Chávez was forced out of bed to appear at the county courthouse in Bakersfield, about thirty miles away. He had been charged with contempt of court for allowing mass picketing at Giumarra's ranch entrances despite a court injunction forbidding it. More than a thousand farm workers accompanied Chávez that day, along with Catholic priests and Protestant clergymen. They jammed into the corridors of the courthouse and knelt on the sidewalks outside in prayer. When Giumarra's lawyers protested and demanded the farm workers' removal from the courthouse, Superior Court Judge Walter Osborne Jr. refused, saying, "If I kick these workers out of this courthouse, that will be just another example of goddamn gringo justice. I can't do it." Citing Chávez's weakened condition, the judge postponed the hearing, but Giumarra's lawyers, realizing they couldn't win, quietly asked the court to dismiss the complaint.

Chávez's twenty-five-day fast came to an end on Sunday, March 10. Some six thousand farm workers and supporters, including Senator Robert Kennedy, were on hand at a Mass of thanksgiving in Delano's Memorial Park. Kennedy and the UFW director had bonded during the Senate subcommittee hearings in 1966 and kept in touch. Assisted by a man on each arm because he was barely able to walk, Chávez ended the fast when "the Senator got a piece of bread and gave it to me."

Chávez's fast had made his point to the union's members. Just as important, he had scored a public relations triumph.

Chávez broke his fast when Senator Robert F. Kennedy (center) handed him a piece of bread. Beside Kennedy is Helen Chávez.

La lucha

······································

The Fight

En Español

10¢

El Malcriado
La Voz del Campesino

Tomo II, Numero 5   Delano, California   miercoles, 1 de mayo, 1968

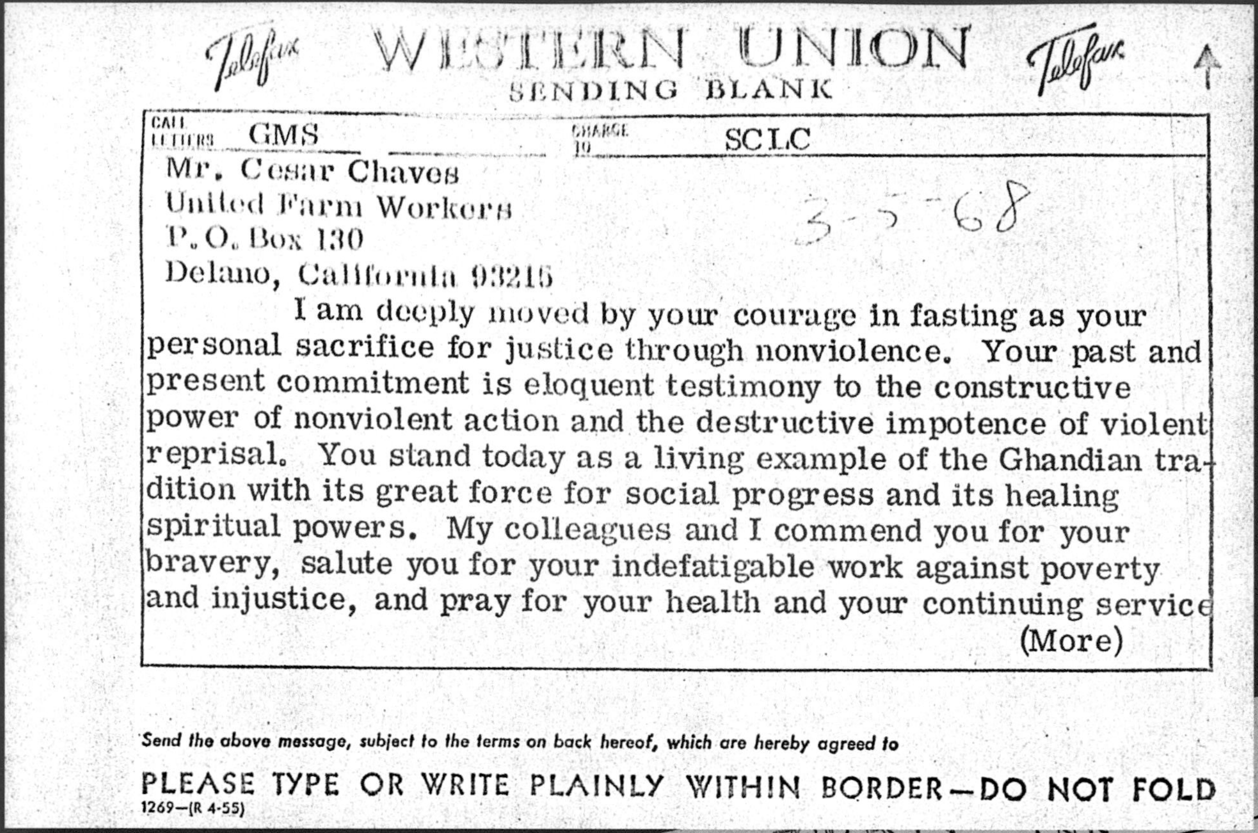

WESTERN UNION

SENDING BLANK

CALL LETTERS GMS — CHARGE TO SCLC

Mr. Cesar Chavez
United Farm Workers
P. O. Box 130
Delano, California 93215

3-5-68

    I am deeply moved by your courage in fasting as your personal sacrifice for justice through nonviolence. Your past and present commitment is eloquent testimony to the constructive power of nonviolent action and the destructive impotence of violent reprisal. You stand today as a living example of the Ghandian tradition with its great force for social progress and its healing spiritual powers. My colleagues and I commend you for your bravery, salute you for your indefatigable work against poverty and injustice, and pray for your health and your continuing service

(More)

Send the above message, subject to the terms on back hereof, which are hereby agreed to

PLEASE TYPE OR WRITE PLAINLY WITHIN BORDER—DO NOT FOLD
1269—(R 4-55)

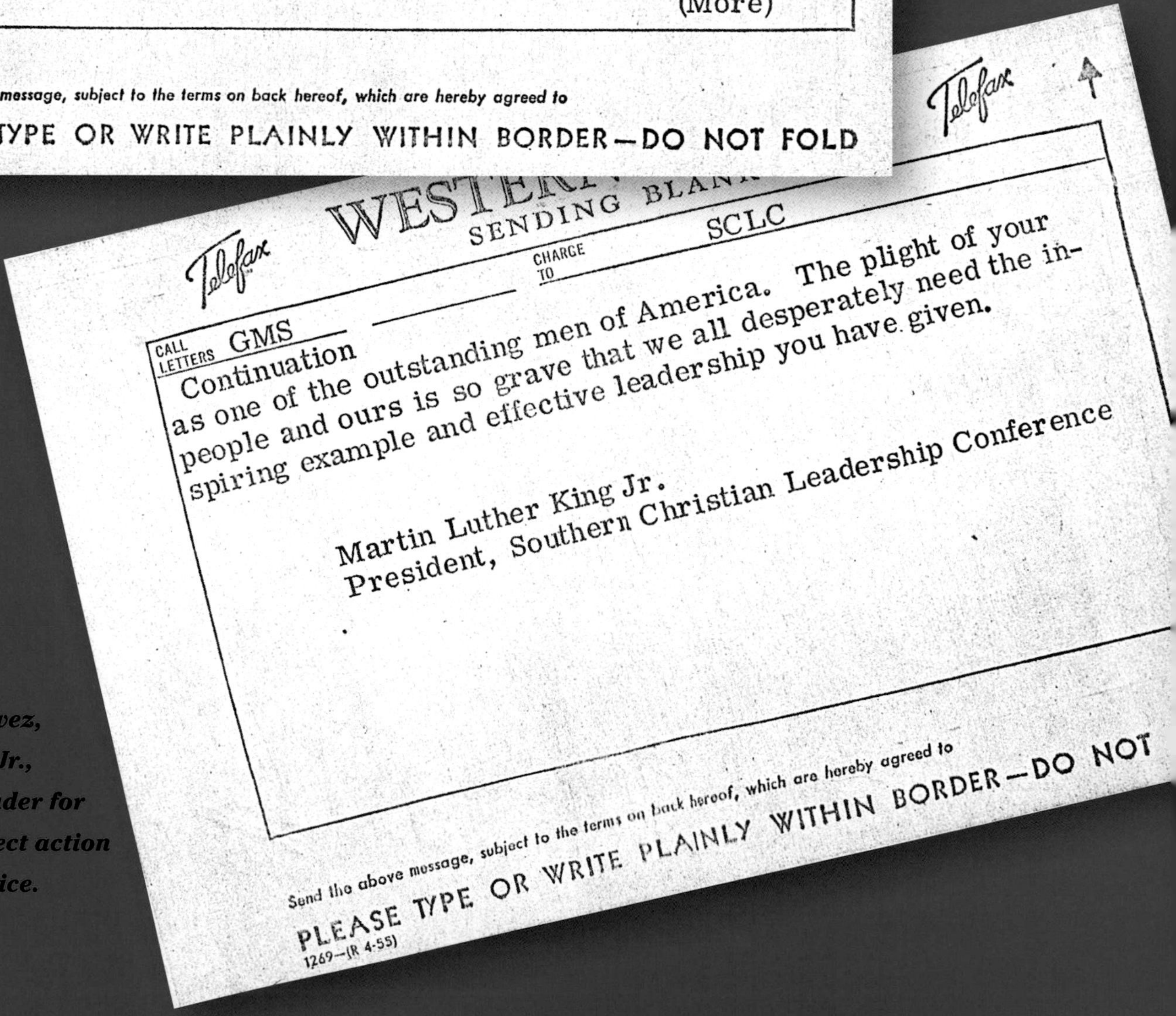

WESTERN UNION SENDING BLANK

CHARGE TO SCLC

CALL LETTERS GMS

Continuation as one of the outstanding men of America. The plight of your people and ours is so grave that we all desperately need the inspiring example and effective leadership you have given.

Martin Luther King Jr.
President, Southern Christian Leadership Conference

Send the above message, subject to the terms on back hereof, which are hereby agreed to

PLEASE TYPE OR WRITE PLAINLY WITHIN BORDER—DO NOT
1269—(R 4-55)

In a telegram to Chávez, Martin Luther King, Jr., praised the labor leader for using nonviolent direct action in the pursuit of justice.

El Doctor Martin Luther King, Jr., fue asesinado en Memphis.

....

Dr. Martin Luther King, Jr., was assassinated in Memphis.

AS 1968 MARCHED ON, THE FARM-WORKER MOVEMENT SEEMED TO FACE DISAPPOINTMENT AFTER DISAPPOINTMENT AND AN UNCERTAIN FUTURE AS TURMOIL AND CHAOS SWEPT THE COUNTRY.

On April 4, the Reverend Dr. Martin Luther King, Jr., was assassinated in Memphis. King, a leader in the civil rights movement since the Montgomery bus boycott of 1955 and 1956, had traveled to that Tennessee city to help striking African American sanitation workers. Earlier, he had sent a telegram to Chávez wishing him and his followers success in their struggle for a better tomorrow. Now on behalf of the UFW, Dolores Huerta sent a note of condolence to the King family and the Southern Christian Leadership Conference, King's civil rights organization. Bayard Rustin, executive director of the A. Philip Randolph Institute (APRI) and King's adviser from the bus boycott until King's death, responded by writing: "Your kind words, encouragement, and offer of support reassured me of the depth

El senador Robert Kennedy fue asesinado apenas dos meses después del asesinato de King.

....

Senator Robert Kennedy was killed just two months after King's assassination.

of your commitment to the struggle for human rights." The APRI was founded by Asa Philip Randolph and Rustin to fight for decent wages, affordable health care, and equality for all Americans. It was Randolph, an African American labor leader and head of the Brotherhood of Sleeping Car Porters, who had the idea for the 1963 March on Washington for Jobs and Freedom, and Rustin, his assistant, helped organize this mass protest.

Following King's assassination, a wave of violence erupted in more than one hundred cities across the United States. In the nation's capital, shock turned to anger and then quickly to violence. Parts of the city were set afire and stores were looted. National guardsmen had to be called in to restore calm. In the end, twelve deaths were linked to the rioting and thousands were injured. More than seven thousand were arrested. After five days, the city was left in desolation.

Senator Robert Kennedy was killed just two months after King's assassination. He had announced his plans to seek the Democratic nomination for president one week after Chávez broke his fast. Kennedy was celebrating his victory in the California primary election when he was shot shortly after midnight on June 5 while leaving through the kitchen of the Ambassador Hotel in Los Angeles. He died early the next morning on June 6— a heartfelt blow to farm workers and Kennedy supporters across the country. "With Senator Robert Kennedy," explained Chávez, "it was like he was ours."

That same year, the farm workers were deeply discouraged by the election of the Republican Party's nominee for president, Richard M. Nixon. Nixon, who was first elected to the U.S. Congress in 1946, had come out early and vocally against the farm-labor movement. Supported by California agribusiness, Nixon had called for numerous investigations into farm-worker unions over the years, calling their leaders pawns of the Communist Party.

In Sacramento, Governor Ronald Reagan, a former actor elected in 1966 and who opposed both the Civil Rights Act of 1964 and the Voting Rights Act of 1965, had long been antiunion despite having been president of the Screen Actors Guild, a labor union for actors. He displayed his disdain for the farm workers' movement by making a show of eating grapes at events held by wealthy supporters. He cast growers as victims, saying, "The farmer has very little bargaining power at harvest time." In December 1968, Reagan called for Congress to pass a law mandating unemployment insurance for all full-time agricultural workers. This proposal, however, would have done nothing for seasonal workers, who made up the vast majority of farm labor. He opposed minimum wage, safety, and workplace standards for farm workers, saying such "benefits [would] increase payroll costs. We cannot serve our California farm workers well by . . . [jeopardizing] the farms which provide these jobs." Joe Gunterman of the Friends Committee on Legislation of California called Reagan's proposals—especially the suggestion to let the state's growers police themselves—"an incredible document—incredibly stupid."

The political opposition facing the UFW was fierce. Despite this, the union stepped up the grape boycott to include supermarkets selling grapes in cities across the United States and Canada, which purchased 20 percent of the California crop. Sit-ins in the middle of stores and pickets outside the entrances disrupted business to such a degree that three chain stores in Toronto eventually removed California grapes from their produce departments, an action followed by the largest grocery chain in Montreal.

In the spring of 1969, the UFW called for a boycott of the West's largest grocery chain, Safeway, which bought 20 percent of Giumarra's table-grape harvest. When Itliong went to company headquarters in Oakland "to discuss the grape boycott and Safeway's million-dollar purchase of scab grapes," he was arrested, along with several other farm workers and volunteers.

By this time, thanks to the attention paid to the peregrinación and his fast, Chávez overshadowed Itliong in the public's eyes, and some AWOC leaders and members complained the UFW was ignoring Filipinos. While Chávez spoke publicly of

Durante años, Nixon había pedido numerosas investigaciones de los sindicatos de trabajadores agrícolas.

Nixon had called for numerous investigations into farm-worker unions over the years.

The UFW and its supporters picketed Safeway stores throughout the West, calling for a boycott until the grocery chain removed grapes from its produce departments.

the UFW as a farm-workers' union, privately he called it his union. Indeed, meetings were often held in Spanish despite complaints from the Filipinos.

Some of Safeway's directors had close ties to California growers. After Itliong's arrest, the company fought back with a $2 million campaign of editorials placed in strategic newspapers and with slogans on bumper stickers. The opinion pieces advocated the rights of the consumer over the lives and welfare of the people who harvested the produce sold in the company's stores. Safeway maintained that it had only the consumers' interests at heart. However, "this argument was disproved by Mrs. Dorothy Kauffman, a Bay Area housewife, who pointed out that over 140,000 consumers feel so strongly against grapes that they have signed petitions refusing to shop at Safeway until the grapes are removed."

While the UFW was boycotting Safeway, the union learned that the U.S. Department of Defense was buying low-priced grapes for troops fighting the war in Vietnam, despite Secretary of Defense Clark Clifford's statement "that one of the principles on which . . . contracts would be based is the contribution [the contracts make] to eradicating poverty." Increasing purchases from fewer than seven million pounds of fresh grapes in 1968 to eleven million pounds in 1969 did little to eliminate poverty among farm workers. New York radio station WMCA editorialized in June 1969 that Defense Department spokesmen gave three reasons for the increased grape shipments: Troop acceptability, a lack of export-quality oranges, and better refrigeration among grape shippers. "We think the Pentagon has taken the *wrong* side. . . . If these are reasons at all, they are reasons why the Pentagon *can* ship more grapes to Vietnam. We have yet to hear one good reason why it *should*." In response to the Department of Defense's policy, the UFW began picketing military facilities across the country.

Most table-grape growers were standing firm with Giumarra in opposing Chávez. Giumarra was steadfast in its refusal to recognize the union. Apparently taking his cue from

"Ésta industria . . . luchará contra Chávez o quién sea para proteger el derecho del público Americano a comer lo que elija comer."

. . . .

"This industry . . . will fight Chavez or anyone else to protect the American public's right to eat what it chooses to eat."

Safeway, Martin Zaninovich, a chief spokesman for the growers, said, "This industry, so long as we must, will fight Chavez or anyone else to protect the American public's right to eat what it chooses to eat when it wishes to do so."

Growers set up the Consumer Rights Committee (CRC), supposedly made up of everyday Americans. The CRC suggested that it was fighting on behalf of the consumers' freedom of choice. In some cities where the UFW was boycotting markets and grocery chains, the CRC established field offices and took out advertising opposing the grape boycott. Hired CRC protesters counterdemonstrated against the UFW. Growers poured a million dollars into the campaign.

Grape producers hit back at the UFW by pressuring the California Farm Bureau Federation to convince Senator George Murphy to sponsor legislation that would make boycotts illegal. They wanted laws that would favor growers in disputes with workers. President Nixon came down squarely in favor of the farm bosses by declaring the boycott unlawful. With "the backing of the John Birch Society [a political group that believes in limited government] and the National Right to Work Committee [which maintains no one should be forced to join or support a union]," Giumarra and other growers decided to set up something they called the Agricultural Workers Freedom to Work Association (AWFWA). They claimed the organization represented workers, but Jerry Cohen discovered that their ranks were filled with growers, field bosses, and labor contractors opposed to the UFW. This was a violation of the law. And, "the Giumarras furnished [AWFWA] office space." Another violation. Fearful that the government would investigate, those behind the AWFWA shut it down.

Growers also fought the UFW with personal attacks on the integrity of its leadership. They claimed Chávez, Itliong, Huerta, and the other union leaders were siphoning off money from workers' dues in order to live in luxury and send their kids to private schools in Switzerland. Like most others who worked full-time for the UFW, Chávez made $5 a week, plus room

Como la mayoría de los que trabajaron a tiempo completo para la UFW, Chávez ganó $5 la semana, además de su alojamiento y comida.

....

Like most others who worked full-time for the UFW, Chávez made $5 a week, plus room and board.

and board. The organization relied heavily on volunteers sympathetic to its cause and on religious groups for food, clothing, and financial contributions. Union recruits, when traveling, stayed with farm workers when possible, with supporters, or in church-owned housing that was typically located in run-down sections of cities and towns where they were sent to organize boycotts.

While the growers fought the UFW with ad campaigns and phantom workers' groups, the union found support from ordinary consumers. Mrs. Florence Klinger, a California resident, asked the state's Democratic senator, Alan Cranston, why the Defense Department had increased its grape purchases during a strike. He responded by saying that he had asked Nixon's secretary of defense Melvin R. Laird, who succeeded Clark Clifford in the position, "for a 'freeze'" on the purchase of grapes. He asked Secretary Laird to return the Defense Department's purchases to the level of 1968 to make sure that the government was truly neutral in its position, as required by law.

Several things occupied Chávez's attention during the summer of 1969. On July 4, growers filed a lawsuit against the UFW claiming $25 million in losses because of the boycott. Cohen plotted strategy against the suit. He found a new line of attack against the growers—their use of pesticides, which workers had complained about for years.

Cohen learned that grape producers were required to register the pesticides they used with county agriculture commissioners. Yet the commissioners refused to give him any details about the chemicals, saying that the information was confidential. Cohen filed suit to obtain the reports.

After winning in court, he learned growers were using a toxic chemical called aldrin. Although farmers diluted it with water before spraying it on crops, in its undiluted form it was deadly within minutes. In order to harvest and tend grapes, field laborers worked under leaves and on ground coated with this and other pesticides, and the chemicals were absorbed into their skin. Upon learning this, boycotters in Washington, D.C., decided to test some grapes they purchased at a local Safeway supermarket. Taking them to a local laboratory, the tests revealed aldrin residue levels that exceeded the limits allowed by the Food and Drug Administration. Now the UFW had a new, potent issue.

On September 29, 1969, Chávez appeared in Washington, D.C., to testify before the Senate Subcommittee on Migratory Labor, where he told senators, "On August 1st, 1969, after testifying concerning the misuse of . . . poisons by table grape growers, our general counsel, Jerry Cohen, submitted to the staff of the Senate Subcommittee . . . a laboratory test from C. W. England Laboratories . . . which indicated that table grapes which were purchased by Manuel Vasquez [a boycotter] at a Safeway store in northeast Washington [D.C.] contained an Aldrin residue of 18 parts per million. Subsequent to that time Senator George Murphy . . . [made] accusations regarding the testimony of the United Farm Workers Organizing Committee . . . [that suggest] the farm workers tampered with the grapes. I can assure you that this is false." In response to the UFW's findings, Safeway conducted its own independent tests. About them, Chávez said, "[Their results] confirmed our tests and [Safeway] . . . cancelled its contract [with the table-grape supplier]."

Chávez told the Senate subcommittee that the use of pesticides posed a danger not only to consumers but also to farm workers. He cited an article in the *Fresno Bee* by Ron Taylor: "An undisclosed number of farm workers are reporting symptoms of pesticide poisoning. Many of these workers do not go to the doctors ordinarily but suffer in silence what they feel is an occupational hazard." Then Chávez told about a three-year-old girl who was playing around an unattended spray rig with her four-year-old brother. Neither the children nor the adult Chicano workers nearby could read English. Curious, the three-year-old stuck her finger into a gallon can of insecticide and then put her finger into her mouth. "She vomited immediately, became unconscious, and was dead on arrival at the hospital where she was promptly taken." Chávez described case after case of mishandled and misused poisons. One of those was that of

OPPOSITE: *At an unidentified location, Itliong (in white hat) rallies pickets calling for the public to support the grape strike.*

*On the brink of a new
harvest in 1970, the grape
strike in the Coachella
Valley continues.*

Gregorio Sisneros, who "was engaged in spraying a vineyard. . . .
According to directions which came with it [the pesticide],
he mixed one quart of . . . poison with a large quantity of water.
But his employer told him to add in another quart of poison,
and so he did. After spraying this mixture a short while he became
ill and had to be taken to a doctor immediately." By the end of

*"Un boicot . . .
cerró por completo
el manejo de
uvas de mesa a
Boston, Nueva York,
Philadelphia,
Chicago, Detroit,
Montreal y Toronto."*

....

"A boycott . . .
closed Boston,
New York,
Philadelphia,
Chicago, Detroit,
Montreal, Toronto
completely
from handling
table grapes."

Chávez's testimony, it was clear that growers had little regard for the safety of their employees. Workers were expendable. The issue was a blow to both Safeway's public relations campaign and the growers who were resisting the boycott.

Support for the boycott mushroomed across North America and even into western Europe, where growers now were trying to sell their crop. More housewives joined college students and farm workers on the boycott lines to pressure markets to remove California grapes from their stock. And they were removed. Lionel Steinberg, a Coachella Valley grape grower, commented, "A boycott of table grapes . . . surprised some growers. . . . [It] literally closed Boston, New York, Philadelphia, Chicago, Detroit, Montreal, Toronto completely from handling table grapes." Pete Velasco, who was in charge of fund-raising for the union, led the labor strike in the Coachella Valley. Although the strike had little impact on many growers because of the availability of scab labor from across the border, the boycott drove some growers out of business. Others cut back on the amount of land under grape cultivation. Steinberg continued, "While before the strike, we had in this little Coachella Valley some two hundred grape growers, in five years we were down to about sixty growers, and where there was once thirteen thousand acres, we were down to seventy-five hundred acres. . . . I was forced to sell some other land that we owned and to heavily mortgage my property to stay in business." The situation in the Coachella Valley wasn't isolated. Throughout California, the boycott was being felt by grape producers.

With the 1970 spring harvest starting up in the Coachella Valley, a committee of Catholic bishops headed by Bishop Joseph Donnelly decided to look into the ongoing strike. They were "interested in bringing the parties together," said Monsignor George Higgins, a member of the committee. They met with growers. And they met with Chávez and his people. The bishops insisted any negotiations they sat in on be serious. A year earlier, negotiations between Steinberg and Huerta broke down at three o'clock in the morning amid shouts and accusations.

*Casi cinco años
de huelgas.
Años de boicots
de consumidores.
Palizas. Arrestos.
Y sacrificios.*

....

Almost five years
of strikes.
Years of consumer
boycotts.
Beatings. Arrests.
And sacrifice.

In early April, Steinberg became the first table-grape grower to negotiate a UFW contract. Other growers soon followed suit as the harvest moved north up the state and into Delano and the Central Valley. For the first time, union contracts with the table-grape industry included language that required employers to provide safety equipment for those working with pesticides as well as warning labels written in Spanish. Those that signed with the union had a distinct advantage over their nonunion competitors, as union-picked table-grape lugs were stamped with the UFW's distinctive label. Major chain grocery stores in the United States and Canada began demanding grapes coming in boxes emblazoned with the union's black eagle.

The strike and boycott had always been about more than simply economics. Monsignor (later Cardinal) Roger Mahony explained, "I don't like to use the word racism, but a feeling really exists between the growers and their Mexican-American workers. . . . They're not used to sitting down and talking with their workers; for decades they've just been telling them this is the way it's going to be. They're not used to dealing with workers on an equal plane."

Almost five years of strikes. Years of consumer boycotts. Beatings. Arrests. And sacrifice. After the first grapes bearing the union label shipped, Giumarra reconsidered its refusal to negotiate. On July 25, 1970, a Saturday, Cohen received a phone call in Delano at around nine o'clock at night. It was the corporation's lawyer, John Giumarra, Jr., nephew of Joseph, the head of the family. He and his father, Joseph's brother, wanted to talk, and right then.

It was one o'clock in the morning of July 26 when Cohen and Chávez met with the Giumarras, father and son, in room forty-four at the Stardust Motel in Delano. By the end of negotiations, grape pickers would receive an immediate hourly pay increase. A committee of growers and workers would be set up to regulate the use of pesticides. And growers would contribute a dime an hour to the medical insurance plan for agricultural workers that the union had established. But the union wanted two more things. First, it wanted the parties to sign the contracts in the UFW's union hall at the Forty Acres. Second—and more important—it wanted the Giumarras to convince the remaining Delano-area growers included in the strike and boycott to sign union contracts, too. The Giumarras said they could deliver that. Even though it was Sunday, by noon the Giumarras persuaded some thirty growers to add their names to the preliminary agreement that had been reached with the union earlier that morning.

Richard Chávez points to the first Coachella Valley grapes to be shipped bearing the union label.

On July 29, Chávez, with Itliong at his side, met with growers at the Forty Acres for the contract signing. The other union officials—Cohen, Huerta, Velasco, Imutan, and Vera Cruz—were all present as well. Farm workers filled the room to witness the historic event, as did Catholic bishops and Protestant clergy who had helped bring the parties together and who had supported the striking workers. Each side offered the other an olive branch, with Giumarra Jr. saying, "It's dawned on everyone in agriculture that unionism has finally come to this industry and there's no sense pretending it will go away. The thing to do is come to the best possible terms." With fingers raised to form the V peace sign, he commented, "If it works here, it can work anywhere."

For his part, Chávez praised nonviolence as the only way to struggle, and said, "This is the beginning of a new day." Adding some humor to the moment, he said that when the two sides met to negotiate, union leaders "were surprised to see the growers did not have horns and I think they were surprised to see that we did not have horns." Speaking about what strikers lost and gained over the course of the lengthy struggle, he commented, "The strikers, and the people involved in the struggle sacrificed a lot, sacrificed all of their worldly possessions. 95% of the strikers lost their homes and their cars. But I think that in losing those worldly possessions they found themselves, and they found that only through dedication, through serving mankind, and in this case, through serving the poor and those who were struggling for justice, only in that way could they really find themselves."

Growers and union leaders exchanged handshakes that bright, sunny Wednesday at the Forty Acres. On both sides, the mood was celebratory as the strike and worldwide boycott of California grapes finally came to an end. Farm workers happily prepared to return to work at higher wages and with workplace protections and considerations unheard of in the past.

Chávez, with Itliong to his right, shakes hands with John Giumarra Jr., signaling the end of the Delano grape strike. John Giumarra Sr. is seated beside his son.

¡Sí, se puede!

Yes, It Can Be Done!

(AFTERWORD)

A Filipino grape picker returns to work in the vineyards at the end of the Delano grape strike.

THE GRAPE STRIKE AND BOYCOTT WAS BUT ONE BATTLE IN THE LONG AND CONTINUING WAR IN THE FIELDS.

The grape strike had drawn media attention for half a decade. Yet it also drew focus away from the thousands of laborers who worked under similarly harsh conditions tending and harvesting California's many other agricultural crops. Even before the ink had dried on the grape contracts, Chávez darted off to the lettuce and vegetable fields around Salinas, along California's central coast. In August and September 1970, thousands of UFW sympathizers and immigrant workers had gone on strike.

Salinas's lettuce growers had observed the UFW's successes in the grape strike and boycott, and they were scared. Eager to end Chávez's influence in their valley, they schemed over the summer with the Teamsters, the old foe of the UFW and the AFL-CIO. The growers secretly signed contracts allowing this union to represent their farm workers. The deal benefited employers more than workers and affected as many as ten thousand laborers in the region's lettuce, carrot, strawberry, tomato, celery, and broccoli fields. However, neither the growers nor the Teamsters told the farm workers anything about the contracts. Yet if the workers didn't want the Teamsters to represent them or if they refused to pay dues to the union, they were fired. This backroom deal denied workers the right to choose who would bargain for them.

OPPOSITE: *In the fall of 1970, the union called for a boycott of nonunion lettuce.*

The Teamsters deal wasn't limited to Salinas. Close to two hundred growers across California and Arizona, hoping to keep the UFW out of the vegetable industry, signed with them, and Itliong called it "a stab in the back of our union." Chávez hadn't planned on another battle with corporate giants, but he had little choice. (Inter Harvest Corporation, a lettuce and vegetable ranch, was owned by the United Fruit Company, a corporation with banana plantations in Central America. Freshpict was owned by Purex, the bleach and cleaning-products company.) Although the UFW filed lawsuits against the grower-Teamster conspiracy, Chávez knew court actions moved slowly. But he wanted to use his strongest weapon, the boycott, only as a last measure. Yet the growers and the Teamsters were doing everything they could to break the UFW's influence over field hands.

The UFW held a rally of twenty-five hundred farm workers at the Hartnell Community College football field on August 2. Before it began, Chávez proclaimed, "No longer can a couple of white men sit down together and write the destinies of all the Chicano and Filipino workers." He was referring to the growers and the Teamster union's top people, nearly all of whom were Anglo and had no experience in field work. Then, in an effort to avert a strike, he called on Governor Ronald Reagan to set up a secret-ballot election so field workers could choose for themselves how they wanted to be represented. The antiunion governor didn't respond.

By the end of the month, growers were physically removing UFW workers from labor camps and firing those who refused to sign cards that authorized the Teamsters union to represent them. On August 23, 1970, most of the remaining workers walked out on strike. Production almost came to a standstill. Normally, 250 railcar loads of lettuce shipped daily. Now it was down to between 62 and 69 railcar loads. Shipments of other vegetables also were down by two-thirds. Tensions were high, so Chávez undertook a six-day fast to restore calm, but the tense atmosphere continued.

Freshpict turned to its friends in the local courts to get an injunction forbidding all picketing. The next day, Chávez

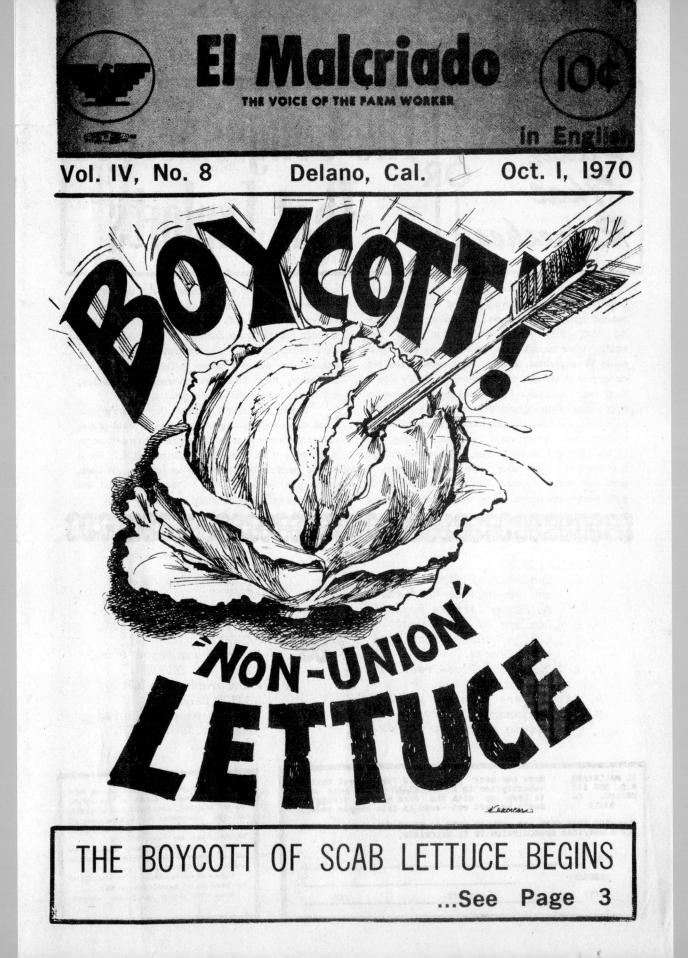

El Malcriado

THE VOICE OF THE FARM WORKER

10¢

in English

Vol. IV, No. 8   Delano, Cal.   Oct. 1, 1970

BOYCOTT!

"NON-UNION" LETTUCE

THE BOYCOTT OF SCAB LETTUCE BEGINS

...See Page 3

called for a ten-day moratorium on the strike, even as he ordered the UFW to prepare to boycott United Fruit's Chiquita banana brand.

Hearing rumors of the planned boycott, one of United Fruit's top executives flew in from the East Coast. He was followed by the chairman of the board of Purex. They seemed willing to negotiate with the UFW to avoid a boycott. But as negotiations got underway, the Teamsters insisted that growers honor their contracts.

Farm workers reacted to the news with anger and shouts of "Huelga!" Almost immediately, the UFW's black-eagle banner was raised on picket lines at fields in Salinas and at ranches up

Chávez . . . mandó que la UFW organizar un boicot contra la marca de plátano Chiquita de United Fruit.

Chávez . . . ordered the UFW to prepare to boycott United Fruit's Chiquita banana brand.

OPPOSITE: *Pickets protest United Fruit's Inter Harvest deal with the Teamsters.*

and down California. Growers got the courts to issue more injunctions. But the picketing continued. The Teamsters, feared because of its often violent history, brought in thugs wielding baseball bats and chains. The growers hired armed guards with shotguns. A ranch foreman drove a bulldozer into strikers' cars, and strikers retaliated with rocks. One picket was shot in the foot. The UFW's Jerry Cohen was hospitalized with a concussion after being beaten during a confrontation with Teamster hoodlums at a struck field. And in Santa Maria, California, 157 miles south of Salinas, where another strike was raging, a UFW picket was arrested for shooting a grower's foreman. Surprising growers and reporters alike, Chávez accepted full blame for the incident and renewed his call for nonviolence.

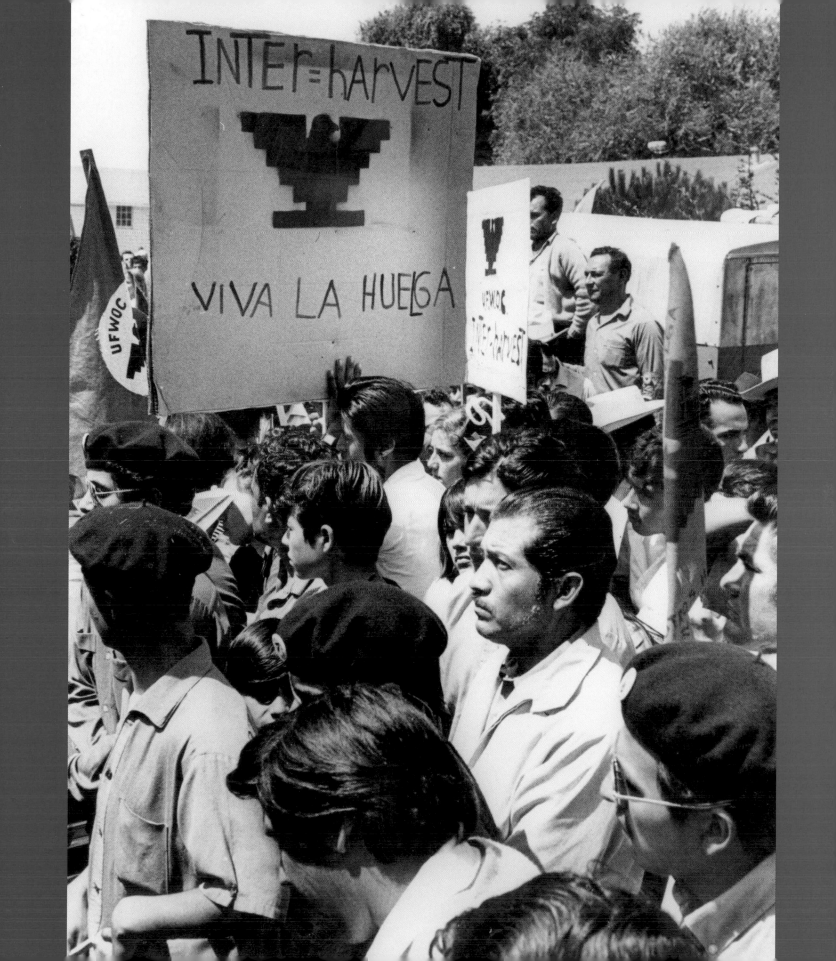

Amid the chaos, however, United Fruit's Inter Harvest canceled its Teamsters contract and negotiated one with the UFW. Compared with the Teamsters agreement, the contract provided improved pay and benefits for farm workers. Also, the new contract eliminated the use of dangerous pesticides, like DDT. Freshpict also signed a UFW contract.

In December 1970, Chávez was arrested and jailed for ignoring a court order to stop boycotting another major lettuce producer in the region, Bud Antle, Incorporated. When Ethel Kennedy, Robert's widow, heard about Chávez's arrest, she decided to show her support by visiting him at the Salinas jail. She was at once surrounded by a hostile, antiunion mob, shouting epithets and spitting on her. Robert Kennedy had seen in Chávez a man who was fighting to lift up the poor, something Kennedy himself had tried to do. The two had formed a strong friendship over talks of politics, religion, and the role of unions in America. After Robert Kennedy's assassination, Chávez remained close to the family. He recognized that the Kennedy brothers—John and Robert—were hugely popular among the Chicano farm workers he was trying to attract and encourage. Many of these laborers adorned their walls with Kennedy photographs displayed next to images of Jesus Christ and the Virgin of Guadalupe. Shortly after Ethel's visit, Chávez was released from jail on Christmas Eve 1970 on orders from the California Supreme Court. It also ruled that the injunction against the boycott and those that had banned the UFW from picketing were unconstitutional.

The union was experiencing victories in the courts and in the fields. But at the same time, there were disagreements among its leadership. Old relationships became strained. In the beginning, the union's members had set policy at the most local level by electing delegates from each ranch to attend the union's convention, held every four years. There, these delegates set overall policy for the UFW; voted on changes to the constitution; elected officers, including the president and members of the executive board; and endorsed political candidates.

OPPOSITE: *Ethel Kennedy, the widow of Robert Kennedy, traveled to the Salinas jail to show her support of Chávez, who had been arrested and imprisoned there.*

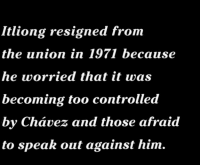

Itliong resigned from the union in 1971 because he worried that it was becoming too controlled by Chávez and those afraid to speak out against him.

Between conventions, the executive board set policies, although important ones still had to be ratified by the delegates at the next convention. Critics now charged that the UFW was becoming less democratic and that Chávez was seizing personal power. In 1971, Itliong resigned from the union, saying, "We in the top echelon of the organization make too many of the rules and we change the rules so very quickly that the workers themselves don't understand what the hell is going on."

Chávez respondió a la ley de Arizona con el comienzo de una nueva huelga de hambre.

....

Chávez responded to the Arizona law by beginning another fast.

To further its identity as a national union, the United Farm Workers Organizing Committee changed its name in 1972 to the United Farm Workers of America. It also moved its headquarters from the Forty Acres in Delano to *Nuestra Señora Reina de la Paz* (Our Lady Queen of Peace), or simply *La Paz*, an abandoned tuberculosis sanatorium located in the mountain town of Keene, California, east of Bakersfield. This move out of the fields of Delano drew more criticism. Some said that it distanced the union from the very people it was supposed to be helping. But it was what Chávez wanted, even over Helen's objections. As a child, she had stayed there briefly, and she didn't want to move back.

Throughout the 1970s and 1980s, the UFW continued the fight for bread and dignity, winning increased wages, more workplace protections, pesticide restrictions, toilets and hand-washing facilities in the fields, and fresh ice water to drink. Negotiators commented that some growers didn't seem to understand why workers needed cold water in the fields where they labored in 110-degree heat, but growers agreed to it. The union won job guarantees, vacation time, and the first-ever pension plan for retired workers. A few growers went so far as to sign contracts that offered profit sharing, something unheard of in the agricultural business.

Yet the union's victories were offset by losses. Agribusinesses spent millions of dollars in farm states to influence legislation and write laws of their own that favored growers and sought to limit the UFW. Arizona, for example, passed a measure in 1972 that banned strikes during harvests and outlawed most boycotts. "We lived with this bill 24 hours a day to get it passed," said the president of the Arizona Farm Bureau Federation (AZFB). "It fulfills an urgent need in the state." The AZFB is an organization that lobbies at the local, state, and federal levels of government on behalf of the state's farmers and ranchers.

Chávez responded to the Arizona law by beginning another fast, in Phoenix, Arizona, on May 11. He was forty-five years old. This hunger strike lasted three and a half weeks, despite doctors' warnings that it could permanently damage his health. A parade of visitors, including Coretta Scott King, widow of the Reverend Dr. Martin Luther King, Jr., supported Chávez in his effort. Out of this fast came the slogan "Sí se puede (Yes, it can be done.)" *Sí, se puede* became the union's rallying cry. As was typical of Chávez, he broke the fast at a Mass attended by thousands of followers and supporters.

Back in Delano, grape growers refused to renegotiate their contracts with the UFW when they expired in 1973. Instead, they signed agreements with the Teamsters. As with the Salinas contracts, these favored growers. So grape workers went out on strike again to show their support of the UFW. Growers reacted with a new round of court injunctions, arrests, and intimidation. Thousands of strikers were arrested for violating antipicketing orders. Hundreds were beaten by Teamster ruffians and law enforcement officers. Two strikers were killed in August, their deaths casting a pall over the entire farm-worker movement.

Mourners carry the casket of Juan de la Cruz in August 1973. He was shot and killed while walking a picket line.

Dos huelguistas fueron asesinados en Agosto.

....

Two strikers were killed in August.

Despite the violence of 1973, the UFW was making strides elsewhere. The Huelga School, the union's school for members' younger children, based at La Paz, was certified as meeting California's educational standards. Also, sixteen union-run service centers around the state were helping workers with housing rental agreements and citizenship classes. Perhaps the most significant achievement was the construction of Agbayani Village, which Itliong and the other Filipino leaders had argued for. Named after a Filipino striker who had died from a heart attack while on a picket line in 1967, the village was a sixty-unit apartment complex at the Forty Acres and built by volunteers. During the 1965 strike, many of the old Filipino workers—those who had come to the United States in the 1920s and 1930s—were thrown out of their camp housing. Because of laws that prevented them from marrying outside their race, they had no families to rely on for support. Now that these men, who were called "uncle" by younger Filipinos and Chicanos alike, were too old to work, Agbayani Village was a place for them to retire, to have a garden, and to live with the security that they wouldn't be evicted.

In Sacramento, the political winds shifted when Democrat Jerry Brown was elected governor in 1974 at the end of Ronald Reagan's two terms. The union had endorsed Brown over his opponent, Republican Houston I. Flournoy, because he seemed friendlier to farm-worker issues. Also, supermarkets, tired of fighting the growers' battles in front of their stores, pressured the agricultural industry to agree to a compromise farm-labor law. Meeting with all the warring parties—growers, the UFW, and the Teamsters—politicians crafted a landmark measure. The California Agricultural Labor Relations Act became law on June 5, 1975, when Brown signed it. It guaranteed farm workers the right to peaceably assemble, freely pick their own union representatives, and bargain with their employers. It also established the Agricultural Labor Relations Board (ALRB) to oversee union elections and to investigate unfair labor practices.

California's agribusinesses disliked the new law. They used their political influence with rural legislators to handpick

The UFW supported the candidacy of Jerry Brown for governor of California. Here, Brown addresses a union rally.

board members sympathetic to big growers and to reduce funding for the ALRB. As a result, the board never lived up to its promise. Growers in farm states throughout the country— but especially in Arizona, Texas, and Florida, where the UFW had made strong inroads among field hands— watched what was happening in California, fearful that a stronger version of the law would come to their states.

It may seem like a small thing, but it was a great victory for farm workers when in 1975 the California Supreme Court overturned a Division of Industrial Safety ruling, and banned el cortito ("the short hoe") from agricultural fields. Growers had argued that without the control of the short hoe, thinning and weeding of crops would be mishandled and they would face

Fue una gran victoria para los trabajadores agrícolas cuando en 1975 el Tribunal Supremo de California . . . prohibió . . . la azada corta.

....

It was a great victory for farm workers when in 1975 the California Supreme Court . . . banned . . . the short hoe.

Chávez in a Philippine rice field

financial loss. Yet California was one of the few states still using the tool. Once again, regulators failed to enforce the Supreme Court ruling until Governor Brown demanded it. State and federal officials held hearings about el cortito's use. One worker who testified challenged them to imagine what using the tool was like by holding the tips of their shoes to approximate the position workers had to assume and then seeing how many times they could walk up and down the length of the room. After that, el cortito was banned from California's fields for good.

Even so, Chávez grew disillusioned with the constant attempts to turn back progress. He complained that for every step forward, they took two steps back. Within the UFW, more of the Filipino leaders who had been the first to leave the fields in 1965 and who had helped the union grow to a nationwide organization also were feeling disappointment. They sensed that they were being ignored. Andy Imutan quit in 1974, although he continued to work with the UFW from time to time. Philip Vera Cruz resigned in 1977 in part because Chávez accepted an invitation to visit the Philippines from its president, Ferdinand Marcos. Reflecting on that trip, Vera Cruz described it as a disgrace; many Filipinos considered Marcos to be a dictator. Indeed, his administration

was marred by corruption, massive repression that included the murders of political opponents, and human rights violations. But what really drove a wedge between Vera Cruz and the UFW director was that Chávez invited Marcos's labor minister to speak at the union's national convention in August 1977. According to Vera Cruz, he rose to speak after the labor minister's comments to challenge what the man had said, but Chávez silenced him. In the union election that followed, Vera Cruz—the last Filipino on the board of directors—didn't even receive a nomination. His position was filled by a Chicano. Of the original 1965 AWOC leaders, only Pete Velasco remained, but he didn't have a leadership role in the UFW.

Many of the Filipinos thought that because Chicanos on the UFW board held Chávez in such high regard, it was difficult for anyone to express an opposing opinion. Also complicating the situation were conflicting views on the direction the union should take. Some wanted the UFW to be a traditional business union concerned mostly about winning better pay, benefits, and work conditions for its members. Others, led by Chávez, wanted the union to take a broader purpose—to address challenges outside the workplace—not only for farm workers but also for other poor people.

Chávez's acquaintance with Charles Dederich, founder of a drug rehabilitation program known as Synanon, also troubled many. What interested Chávez most about Dederich was a treatment technique used at Synanon called the Game. It was a group session that allowed everyone to speak freely about each other. Often these sessions turned into shouting matches and involved personal attacks. Chávez thought it might help improve communication and problem solving among the union's leadership. He also liked the way Dederich and the addicts he treated all lived together, communally. This was something he was encouraging at La Paz.

Synanon had some success and Dederich became wealthy because of government contracts that sent addicts to his facility in Santa Monica, California. Yet the program also had a dark side. Over time, Synanon evolved into a cult, with Dederich as an authoritative and dangerous leader. Female addicts were forced to shave their heads to show their obedience to him, and males were required to undergo sterilization. Couples were required to divorce. Those who opposed Dederich became enemies and were forced out of Synanon—something he encouraged Chávez to do with disloyal union leadership—or they were beaten. In 1980, Dederich was sentenced to five years in jail for conspiracy to commit murder after his followers stuffed a rattlesnake into the mailbox of a lawyer who had successfully sued Synanon on behalf of a former member.

When Chávez introduced the Game at La Paz, he was surprised to find himself the target of criticism. His staff members directed their anger at him. One of his sons, Paul, verbally attacked Chávez for his long absences when Paul was a child. Ultimately, instead of improving communication, the Game deepened divisions. Some chose to leave rather than be subjected to the forced humiliation. Writing about this time in UFW history, Caitlin Flanagan's June 13, 2011, article in *The Atlantic*, "The Madness of Cesar Chavez," and Miriam Pawel's well-researched book, *The Union of Their Dreams: Power, Hope, and Struggle in Cesar Chavez's Farm Worker Movement*, suggest that Chávez purged or exiled those who disagreed with him, those whom he considered to be traitors to the union. He also began to hold farm workers in contempt. Flanagan writes, "His desire was not to lift workers into the middle class, but to bind them to one another in the decency of sacrificial poverty." This was the life he had chosen for himself and the one he had chosen for the union's leadership. Cohen had urged Chávez to pay the organizers and directors professional salaries in order to keep good talent and help them raise their families. Because of this stand, according to Pawel, Cohen was forced out. And in a tape-recorded meeting at La Paz, Chávez is quoted as saying, "Every time we look at them [the farm workers], they want more money. Like pigs, you know." Whether saint or flawed hero, Chávez became more isolated from those in the fields and more inflexible in his handling of the union.

Chávez—con sesenta y un años—empezó una nueva huelga de hambre y juró no volver a comer hasta que los productores quitaran los pesticidas de sus campos.

....

Chávez—at age sixty-one—undertook a new fast and vowed not to eat until growers removed pesticides from their fields.

Controversy notwithstanding, the UFW continued to grow in the early 1980s. At its peak, the union counted some fifty thousand to sixty thousand dues-paying members across the United States. Despite the Filipinos' departure from the union and from leadership, in 1980, Pete Velasco, the remaining Filipino leader, was elected to the union's second-highest office, secretary-treasurer, a position he held until his retirement in 1988. The union's numbers alone forced some growers to reexamine their business practices with a conscience. A few conceded that they would have to work closer with the people in their fields and be fairer in their treatment of them.

Also during this time, the UFW increased its focus on pesticides after it noticed that groups of cancer victims, mostly children, were concentrated in the small farm towns around California's Central Valley. Aircraft that dusted crops with toxic chemicals sometimes sprayed workers in the fields or vehicles passing along the roads nearby. Also, it wasn't unusual for laborers to enter fields only moments after they'd been treated. Chávez, as well as many in the medical profession, believed the cancers were caused by chemicals used on crops. In the summer of 1984, he called for the third boycott of grapes to protest the use of these poisons.

In 1986, Chávez learned that growers sometimes combined pesticides. Nobody knew the effects of these chemical combinations because they were untested. The UFW shed light on this practice, and the state launched an investigation. In the end, the growers agreed to quit mixing chemicals in unapproved ways.

Hoping to draw attention to the industry's use and misuse of chemicals, Chávez—at age sixty-one—undertook a new fast and vowed not to eat until growers removed pesticides from their fields. After thirty-six days, the end of the fast was announced by his son Fernando on August 21, 1988. A crowd of eight thousand attended a Mass under a tent at the Forty Acres. He had returned to the old UFW headquarters in Delano because it was more convenient for field hands to reach and because that was where the farm workers' struggle began.

Cada vez que expiraban los contratos de los sindicatos, comenzaban de nuevo las batallas con los productores.

Every time union contracts expired, there were renewed battles with growers.

As the 1990s began, Chávez cut back on his public appearances. The UFW's focus on pesticides rather than the real work of unions—wages and benefits—had caused some rank-and-file members to leave the organization. Farm workers couldn't measure a healthier work environment in the same way they could a pension or medical plan. Even so, Chávez pushed forward with plans for a renewed grape boycott to protest pesticide use. Also, it seemed that every time union contracts expired, there were renewed battles with growers, and the fights seemed to be sapping the energy of both the general membership and of Chávez. In October 1990, Helen and the family persuaded him to accept an invitation from the Coachella Valley to celebrate the opening of a new school bearing his name, his first public honor. Then on December 14, 1991, his ninety-nine-year-old mother, Juana Estrada Chávez, died in San Jose. It was a serious blow that took him some time to recover from. His mother's death was followed on September 27, 1992, with the death at eighty-two of his mentor and friend of forty years, Fred Ross.

In April 1993, Chávez was in Yuma, Arizona, not far from his boyhood home, to testify in a lawsuit brought by Bruce Church Incorporated over losses sustained during the UFW lettuce boycott in the 1980s. Church was an agribusiness giant in Salinas, with land holdings in both California and Arizona. (In a strange twist of circumstances, its holdings included the Yuma ranch were Chávez had grown up.) Church had chosen to file its lawsuit in Arizona because this conservative state had laws forbidding boycotts and it was friendly to growers.

On April 22, after two days of exhausting court testimony, Chávez drove to a friend's home in nearby San Luis to spend the night. He seemed to be in a cheerful mood, but he admitted that he was tired. Retiring to bed, he died in his sleep during the early morning hours on April 23, 1993. He was sixty-six years old.

Chávez, who never earned more than $5,000 a year, had wished for a simple burial, and his family honored that request. He was buried in a plain pine casket built by Richard. Thousands of mourners joined the three-mile-long funeral procession on

April 29 through Delano to the Forty Acres. It was their last march with the Chicano civil rights and labor leader. Chávez's body was buried in a rose garden at union headquarters at La Paz.

On August 8, 1994, the Presidential Medal of Freedom, America's highest civilian award, was given to Chávez posthumously by President Bill Clinton. Chávez's wife, Helen, accepted the award in a White House ceremony. In 1996, the $3 million judgment against the UFW won by Bruce Church Incorporated was thrown out by a state appeals court. The company signed a UFW contract in May 1996. On October 8, 2012, before seven thousand people, President Barack Obama dedicated the site in Keene as the César E. Chávez National Monument.

Over the years, UFW membership has declined to around five thousand, and union contracts have fallen off as well. Working conditions in many fields have gotten worse as the union's influence has shrunk.

Still, the work of the union Chávez founded moves ahead with an eye to the future. The organization is looking again at its founding idea: that is, a union of and by farm workers. Also, through the Cesar Chavez Foundation, established by Chávez's family to continue his memory, the compassion and generosity he learned from his mother so long ago influences future generations. The foundation provides affordable housing in four states for low- and very-low-income farm workers, families, and seniors and offers educational programs for adults and disadvantaged youth.

The idea of starting a union to improve the lives of farm workers may have seemed almost impossible in 1962, but Chávez—aided by Itliong and the Filipinos who refused to accept wages lower than those for imported workers—proved that through faith, perseverance, and nonviolent direct action, it can be done.

¡Sí, se puede!

Actor and activist James Edward Olmos (center) and Congressman Joseph Kennedy, son of Robert F. Kennedy, (behind Olmos) help carry the simple pine casket bearing the body of Chávez along the funeral procession in Delano, California, April 29, 1993.

AUTHOR'S NOTE

César Chávez . . . era y es una figura polémica.

César Chávez . . . was, and is, a controversial figure.

César Chávez . . . was, and is, a controversial figure.

OPPOSITE: *Filipinos came to the mainland of the United States to prosper, but most ended up working in the farm fields.*

I came to *STRIKE!* by way of the classroom, where I first became aware of the gulf between the haves and the have-nots in agriculture when I began teaching high school in the mid-1970s in El Centro, California. In my classroom, I taught growers' children as well as children of field workers, the latter mostly Mexican American. Outside of class, the two groups rarely mixed.

Many of the Mexican American students I taught were enrolled only while their parents worked in Imperial Valley's vegetable fields. When the crops were harvested, the families moved north to the Salinas Valley. Even when enrolled, the students were frequently absent because they needed to look after younger brothers and sisters so their parents could work, or worked themselves—illegally, because most were underage. At one point, concerned (and a little irritated) because some of my students were falling behind and not turning in their homework, I made a home visit. From the outside, the building I went to that afternoon at the edge of a sugar beet field looked a little shabby and worn. When I knocked on the door, I discovered three families of migrant workers living in a small, two-room apartment. Their electricity had been shut off because they were unable to pay the bill. Homework—or the lack thereof—suddenly seemed unimportant. The incident stirred in me a lifelong interest in the lives of this often invisible part of America.

César Chávez was one who'd experienced the migrant farm-worker life and knew inside and out what field laborers faced. Yet he was, and is, a controversial figure. At once a hated and loved man, depending on which side of the field one is from, he and the union he headed won history-making concessions from California's agricultural growers. From toilet and hand-washing facilities in the fields to medical and pension plans to better wages, the United Farm Workers helped field hands achieve a little dignity and respect from an industry that had always treated them badly and undervalued the labor that brought food to American tables and profits to corporate farmers. Despite this, Chávez is often criticized because of the credit he took for the 1965 grape strike. What's more, those close to him often have kept alive and even exaggerated that credit. To read books about the fight in the fields usually means reading the biography of César Chávez. The work of Larry Itliong, the Filipino organizer of the Agricultural Workers Organizing Committee, which predates the National Farm Workers Association, is mentioned only in passing or forgotten altogether. One must ask: if Itliong and AWOC had not put down their tools on September 8, 1965, would Chávez be the icon he is today?

Supporters point to his reputation for including people of all walks, from college students to clergy. The union Chávez helped found along with his wife, Helen, Dolores Huerta, Gilbert Padilla, and others seemed to welcome everybody. Despite this, he viewed undocumented workers, especially those from Mexico, as the competition and as strikebreakers who likely would take jobs away from union members. On more than one occasion, critics say, he or his staff called the Immigration and Naturalization Service to report these workers so they would be picked up and returned to Mexico. Critics point to UFW-funded business ventures that were completed using nonunion labor, and a pension plan of at least $100 million that very few farm workers qualify to benefit from. Some complained of nepotism, suggesting the UFW was and is little more than a family-run business that provided jobs to close relatives and favored friends. For more about this side of Chávez and the UFW, I suggest Miriam Pawel's *The Union of Their Dreams* and Matt Garcia's *From the Jaws of Victory*.

For me, the most troubling aspect of Chávez was his relationship with Synanon founder Charles Dederich and Dederich's apparent influence over him. Chávez had to be aware of Synanon's evolution

La peregrinación y su primera huelga de hambre . . . elevó a Chávez a tal punto que eclipsó a todos los demás en el sindicato.

. . . .

The pilgrimage and Chávez's first fast . . . raised Chávez to a point where he overshadowed everyone else in the union.

into a cult, as it was well reported in the media of the day. Multiple sources maintained that after they struck up a friendship, Chávez became more of a loner, more likely to do things his way, and more inclined to surround himself with a board of directors that would approve. The friendship also came at a time when the strong union of the 1970s and early 1980s was losing its influence in the fields. Chávez held on to his position in the UFW until he died. Still, I have to ask if the union might have continued to be a strong force for agricultural labor if only he had had people around him who were willing to oppose him when it was necessary.

The critics' views notwithstanding, Chávez deserves credit for a lot of accomplishments, but he didn't achieve them alone. When news came out that I was working on a nonfiction book about the 1965 grape strike, I received several phone calls and e-mails from Filipino Americans asking me to remember Itliong and AWOC's contributions to the farm-worker movement. I've tried to do that here to the best of my ability, given that not many of the original AWOC leaders told their stories or left behind anything more than the day-to-day running of the union—and even that was sketchy. To my knowledge, Philip Vera Cruz is the only one of the original leaders who went out on strike to have written about his time in AWOC and the UFW. Johnny Itliong helped with remembrances of his father, but he was a child at the time of the strike and his memories are shaded by youth and time. Dolores Velasco gave me a box of clippings and other information her late husband, Pete, had kept. While helpful, most of the materials focused on Chávez, as did newspaper articles after the NFWA merged with AWOC, and especially after the pilgrimage and Chávez's first fast. These two defining events raised Chávez to a point where he overshadowed everyone else in the union. So while I have done my best to write about the Filipino role in the grape strike and hope I have

At the end of the pilgrimage from Delano to Sacramento, union supporters crowd the state capitol plaza.

done it and the individuals involved justice, I know there was more to their story.

In *STRIKE!* I took the liberty of referring to Filipino Americans as *Filipinos* because this was the language of the time and the term Filipino Americans used to refer to themselves. I also referred to Mexican nationals as *Mexicans*, while referring to Mexican Americans either as *Mexican Americans* or *Chicanos*, depending on the chronology. In the 1960s, Mexican Americans began calling themselves *Chicanos* rather than the current term, *Latinos*. My use of these terms was done with the best of intentions and with the greatest respect.

Numerous resources were used in writing *STRIKE!* Among those that were critical to my understanding of the farm-worker movement, camp conditions, and in particular the 1965 Delano grape strike and subsequent years were *The Fight in the Fields: Cesar Chavez and the Farmworkers Movement* by Susan Ferriss and Ricardo Sandoval, edited by Diana Hembree; *The Fight in the Fields: Cesar Chavez and the Farmworkers' Struggle*, a documentary film by Ray Telles and Rick Tejada-Flores; *Cesar Chavez: Autobiography of La Causa* by Jacques E. Levy; *The Words of César Chávez*, edited by Richard J. Jensen and John C. Hammerback; *Cesar Chavez: An Organizer's Tale: Speeches*, edited by Ilan Stavans; *The Union of Their Dreams: Power, Hope, and Struggle in Cesar Chavez's Farm Worker Movement* by Miriam Pawel; and *The Original Writings of Philip Vera Cruz* by Sid Amores Valledor.

Several documentary films, in addition to *The Fight in the Fields* cited above, also proved useful: *Fighting for Our Lives* (1974) by Glen Pearcy, Peter Matthiessen, and Luis Valdez for the United Farm Workers; "Harvest of Shame," a 1960 documentary by *CBS Reports* and reported by Edward R. Murrow; *Dollar a Day, Ten Cents a Dance* (1984) by

-DON SOTACO-

George Ow Jr., directed by Geoffrey Dunn and Mark Schwartz; *Decision at Delano* (1967) by Jack L. Copeland for Jack Copeland Productions; *Wrath of Grapes* (1987) by the United Farm Workers; and *Common Man, Uncommon Vision: The Cesar Chavez Story* (1995) by Dana Dunnells and Ronald Gordon for ZGS Communications.

Newspaper resources also helped shed light on attitudes and events as they were unfolding. These included numerous accounts from *El Malcriado*, the *Los Angeles Times*, the *New York Times*, the *Washington Post*, the *Fresno Bee*, and the *Boston Globe*. Personal recollections, diaries, letters, FBI files, and other documents (including a hate-filled death threat against Chávez), held at the Walter P. Reuther Library, Archives of Labor and Urban Affairs, Wayne State University, and Chávez's oral history, held at the John F. Kennedy Library, also were instrumental in helping me shape the book before you. Finally, recorded interviews that I conducted in January 2013 with Paul Chávez, Chávez's middle son, and Dolores Velasco, widow of Pete Velasco, were invaluable sources of information, insight, and understanding, as was my discussion with Bernadette Farinas, one of Chávez's granddaughters.

As Chávez and the vice presidents canvassed the Central Valley for union members, workers—portrayed by artist Andy Zermeño as Don Sotaco—had to decide whether to risk joining the union.

1898	The Philippines becomes a possession of the United States.
1904	Philip Vera Cruz is born on December 25.
1910	Pete Velasco is born on August 18.
1913	Larry Itliong is born on October 25 in San Nicolas, Pangasinan, Philippines.
1926	Philip Vera Cruz arrives in the United States. Andy Imutan is born on March 8.
1927	Césario Estrada Chávez is born on March 31 in Yuma, Arizona.
1929	Mexican Repatriation begins by local, state, and federal authorities and continues through 1939. Itliong arrives in the United States.
1930	Dolores Huerta is born on April 10 in Dawson, New Mexico.
1931	Velasco comes to the United States.
1937	The Chávez family loses its Yuma, Arizona, ranch.
1939	The Chávez ranch is auctioned off by the state.
1942	The Mexican Farm Labor Program, also known as the *bracero* program, begins.
1947	Fred Ross founds the Community Service Organization (CSO).
1952	Chávez meets Fred Ross and joins the CSO.
1955	Huerta joins the CSO. She meets Chávez a year later through Ross.
1959	Itliong and Huerta found the Agricultural Workers Organizing Committee (AWOC).
1960	The day after Thanksgiving, *CBS Reports* broadcasts Edward R. Murrow's "Harvest of Shame."
1962	Chávez leaves the CSO on March 31 to establish the National Farm Workers Association (NFWA). On September 30, it holds its founding convention in Fresno.
1964	*El Malcriado*, the voice of the farm worker and a publication of the NFWA, debuts in December.
1965	In March, the NFWA successfully negotiates with rose growers in McFarland, California. AWOC negotiates better wages for grape pickers in California's Coachella Valley in May. September 8, Filipino workers strike Delano vineyards. They are joined by the NFWA on September 20. In October, *El Teatro Campesino*, the farm workers' theater, is launched.

1966	In March, the Senate Subcommittee on Migratory Labor holds hearings at Delano High School.
	On March 17, Chávez leads the march from Delano to Sacramento.
	In August, the NFWA and AWOC merge to become the United Farm Workers Organizing Committee (UFW).
1967	On August 3, Chávez calls for a strike against the Giumarra Vineyards and a boycott of its products.
1968	On February 15, Chávez begins a fast for nonviolence. It ends on March 10.
	In April, the Reverend Martin Luther King, Jr., is assassinated.
	This is followed in June by the assassination of Senator Robert F. Kennedy.
1969	UFW investigates pesticides and their impact on consumers and farm workers.
1970	UFW signs contracts with Giumarra and the remaining Delano grape growers, bringing an end to the grape strike and boycott. In August and September, workers go on strike in Salinas, California.
1971	Itliong quits the UFW.
1972	UFW changes its name to the United Farm Workers of America. Arizona passes restrictive farm-labor laws.
	Chávez fasts in Phoenix to protest.
1973	Delano grape growers refuse to negotiate with the UFW when their contracts expire.
	Instead, the growers turn to the Teamsters.
1974	Imutan leaves the UFW.
1975	California passes the Agricultural Labor Relations Act in June and establishes a board to oversee farm-labor practices.
	El cortito is banned.
1977	Itliong dies on February 8 in Delano, California. Philip Vera Cruz resigns from the UFW.
1988	Chávez fasts for thirty-six days to draw attention to the use of pesticides.
1993	On April 23, Chávez dies in Yuma, Arizona.
1994	The Presidential Medal of Freedom is given posthumously to Chávez. Vera Cruz dies.
1995	Velasco dies on December 1.
2011	Imutan dies on February 2.
2012	President Barack Obama dedicates the César E. Chávez National Monument in Keene, California, site of the UFW headquarters.

FOR MORE INFORMATION

BOOKS

Alinsky, Saul D. *Rules for Radicals: A Pragmatic Primer for Realistic Radicals*. New York: Vintage Books, 1989.

Bardacke, Frank. *Trampling Out the Vintage: Cesar Chavez and the Two Souls of the United Farm Workers*.
New York: Verso Books, 2011.

Doak, Robin S. *Dolores Huerta: Labor Leader and Civil Rights Activist*. Minneapolis: Compass Point Books, 2008.

Dunne, John Gregory. *Delano: The Story of the California Grape Strike*. Berkeley: University of California Press, 2008.

Ferriss, Susan, and Ricardo Sandoval. *The Fight in the Fields: Cesar Chavez and the Farmworkers Movement*.
Edited by Diana Hembree. Orlando, FL: Harcourt Brace (Paradigm Productions), 1997.

Garcia, Matt. *From the Jaws of Victory: The Triumph and Tragedy of Cesar Chavez and the Farm Worker Movement*.
Berkeley: University of California Press, 2012.

Gillis, Jennifer Blizin. *Dolores Huerta*. Chicago: Heinemann Library, 2006.

Jensen, Richard J., and John C. Hammerback, eds. *The Words of César Chávez*. College Station: Texas A&M
University Press, 2002.

Kallen, Stuart A. *We Are Not Beasts of Burden: Cesar Chavez and the Delano Grape Strike*. Minneapolis: Twenty-First Century
Books, 2011.

Krull, Kathleen. *Harvesting Hope: The Story of Cesar Chavez*. Illustrated by Yuyi Morales. San Diego: Harcourt, 2003 (picture book).

Levy, Jacques E. *Cesar Chavez: Autobiography of La Causa*. Minneapolis: University of Minnesota Press, 2007.

Matthiessen, Peter. *Sal Si Puedes (Escape If You Can): Cesar Chavez and the New American Revolution*. Berkeley: University
of California Press, 2000 (paperback edition). First published 1969.

Miller, Debra A. *Dolores Huerta: Labor Leader*. Detroit: Thomson Gale, 2007.

Nahmias, Rick. *The Migrant Project: Contemporary California Farm Workers*. Albuquerque: University of New Mexico Press, 2008.

Nelson, Eugene. *Huelga! The First Hundred Days of the Great Delano Grape Strike*. Delano, CA: Farm Worker Press, 1966.

Orosco, José-Antonio. *Cesar Chavez and the Common Sense of Nonviolence*. Albuquerque: University of New Mexico Press, 2008.

Pawel, Miriam. *The Union of Their Dreams: Power, Hope, and Struggle in Cesar Chavez's Farm Worker Movement*.
New York: Bloomsbury Press, 2009.

Scharlin, Craig, and Lilia V. Villanueva. *Philip Vera Cruz: A Personal History of Filipino Immigrants and the Farmworkers Movement*.
Seattle: University of Washington Press, 2000.

Shaw, Randy. *Beyond the Fields: Cesar Chavez, the UFW, and the Struggle for Justice in the 21st Century*.
Berkeley: University of California Press, 2010 (reprint edition).

Soto, Gary. *Cesar Chavez: A Hero for Everyone*. Illustrated by Lori Lohstoeter. New York: Aladdin Books, 2003 (picture book).

Stavans, Ilan, ed. *Cesar Chavez: An Organizer's Tale; Speeches*. New York: Penguin, 2008.

Stavans, Ilan. *Cesar Chavez: A Photographic Essay*. El Paso, TX: Cinco Puntos Press, 2010.

Valledor, Sid Amores. *The Original Writings of Philip Vera Cruz*. Indianapolis, IN: Dog Ear Publishing, 2006.

Van Tol, Alex. *Dolores Huerta: Voice for the Working Poor*. St. Catharines, ON: Crabtree Publishing, 2011.

Warren, Sarah E. *Dolores Huerta: A Hero to Migrant Workers*. Illustrated by Robert Casilla. Tarrytown, NY: Marshall Cavendish Children, 2012 (picture book).

Worth, Richard. *Dolores Huerta*. New York: Chelsea House, 2007.

WEBSITES*

America's Story from America's Library (Library of Congress).
americaslibrary.gov/aa/chavez/aa_chavez_subj.html

"An American Hero: The Biography of César E. Chávez" (California Department of Education).
chavez.cde.ca.gov/ModelCurriculum/Teachers/Lessons/Resources/Biographies/K-2_Bio.aspx

Cesar Chavez.biography. Biography.com.
biography.com/people/cesar-chavez-9245781

Cesar Chavez Foundation.
chavezfoundation.org

Farmworker Movement Documentation Project.
farmworkermovement.us

United Farm Workers.
ufw.org

PLACES TO VISIT

César E. Chávez National Monument
29700 Woodford-Tehachapi Road
Keene, California 93531
nps.gov/cech/index.htm

The Forty Acres National Historic Landmark
30168 Garces Highway
Delano, California 93215
nps.gov/history/nr/travel/american_latino_heritage/The_Forty_Acres.html

Websites active at time of publication

ACKNOWLEDGMENTS

Researching *STRIKE!* was rewarding and challenging and frustrating. The rewards came in the form of people who opened their doors to me, were patient with my questions, and shared their personal recollections of César Chávez and those early days when Filipino Americans began the Delano grape strike. Others sent me information long after my research visit in the hope that it might be useful to my writing (It was!). And still others trusted that I would return borrowed materials that I carried back to my home in Tucson, Arizona. At the same time, I was challenged by the sheer volume of information available about the grape strike and its key Chicano players. So much information was available—from FBI files to diaries to correspondence and newspaper clippings. Usually, this is a good problem to have because I love doing research. But I was overwhelmed. Yet I also felt an obligation to sift through it all, even if I knew that most of it would never make it into the final book. Still another challenge was the weather; temperatures that dipped to two below zero made my treks to Detroit's Reuther Library a bone-chilling experience for a desert resident like me. I was also frustrated by the lack of acknowledgment of and information about the Filipinos who had begun the strike and who worked for years beside Chávez to see it succeed.

First and foremost, I wish to thank the Cesar Chavez Foundation for allowing me access to its collection of materials and for arranging guided tours of La Paz and the Forty Acres. I owe thanks to a great many people who gave of their time and knowledge. They are Paul Chávez, Chávez's middle son and president of the Cesar Chavez Foundation; Bernadette Farinas, Chávez's granddaughter; and Dolores Velasco, widow of UFW secretary-treasurer Pete Velasco; Sheila Geivet and Norberto Vargas for walking the Forty Acres with me and pointing out things that aren't included in the history books, such as the small space above the service bay where Chávez hid when threats on his life were made; William LeFevre, reference archivist, Kathleen Emery Schmeling, archivist, and Elizabeth Murray Clemens, audio-visual archivist, Walter P. Reuther Library, Archives of Labor and Urban Affairs; Sam Rubin, archivist and educator, John F. Kennedy Library; Melissa Scroggins, librarian, California History and Genealogy Room, Fresno County Public Library; Marc Grossman, Chávez's longtime personal aide and press secretary, and communications director, Cesar Chavez Foundation, for vetting my manuscript and offering a thorough review of the first draft (which was really closer to the twenty-second draft); Pam Muñoz Ryan, Kendra Marcus, and especially Lawrence Schimel for Spanish translations when my own Spanish felt too rusty to be trusted; Jim Patrick, Information Services Department, Yuma County Main Library; Johnny Itliong, son of Larry Itliong; Gloria Washington, reference librarian, Kern County Public Library; Aryn Glazier, photo services, Dolph Briscoe Center for American History, University of Texas, Austin; Jan Grenci, reference specialist–posters, Prints and Photographs Division, Library of Congress; Guy Porfirio, illustrator, guyporfirio.com; Shelly Longoria, librarian, Palm Springs Public Library; Kay Peterson, Archives Center, Smithsonian Institution; and finally and not least of all my editor, Carolyn P. Yoder, and the entire Calkins Creek team—I couldn't do it without your patience, support, and guidance. Heartfelt thanks to all.

SOURCE NOTES*

CHAPTER 1   page 8

"Field Strike Idles . . .": *Fresno Bee*, September 9, 1965, p. 6D.

"Growers say 500 . . .": "Field Workers' Strike Moves into Sixth Day," *Bakersfield Californian*, September 13, 1965, p. 34.

"slave labor wages . . .": Jim Smith, "Hundreds Cheer Strike Plans at Delano Meeting," *Bakersfield Californian*, September 15, 1965, p. 12.

"We're going to march . . .": Ibid.

"We have not . . .": George Meany, letter to Mrs. Franklin D. Roosevelt, Archives of Labor and Urban Affairs, Walter P. Reuther Library, Wayne State University.

"workers stayed off . . .": "Mexican Farm Workers Expected in State Soon," by Harry Bernstein, *Los Angeles Times*, May 11, 1965.

"on charges of . . .": Ibid.

"on suspicion of . . .": Ibid.

"The victory . . .": Andy Imutan, "What Happened When Mexicans and Filipinos Joined Together," United Farm Workers, ufw.org/_page.php?menu=research&inc=history/04.html (accessed May 8, 2013).

"We knew then that . . .": Ibid.

"I was surprised . . .": Jacinto Sequig, *Dollar a Day, Ten Cents a Dance* (documentary film), by George Ow Jr., Impact Productions, 1984.

"The Filipino decision . . .": "A Farm Worker's Viewpoint," by Philip Vera Cruz, Archives of Labor and Urban Affairs, Walter P. Reuther Library.

* Websites active at time of publication

"men who work . . .": "Imperialism in Our Fields," by Henry Anderson, director of research, Agricultural Workers Organizing Committee, AFL-CIO, 1961, Archives of Labor and Urban Affairs, Walter P. Reuther Library.

"Through the last one hundred . . .": "Human Resources and California Agriculture," statement prepared by the Agricultural Workers Organizing Committee, AFL-CIO, 1959, Archives of Labor and Urban Affairs, Walter P. Reuther Library.

"Mexican workers started crossing . . .": Andy Imutan, "What Happened When Mexicans and Filipinos Joined Together," United Farm Workers, ufw.org.

"There are Mexicans . . .": Pete Velasco, *The Fight in the Fields: Cesar Chavez and the Farmworkers' Struggle* (documentary film), by Ray Telles and Rick Tejada-Flores, a Paradigm Production, distributed by the Cinema Guild, 2004.

CHAPTER 2   page 26

"at least 180 . . .": César Chávez, *Cesar Chavez: Autobiography of La Causa*, by Jacques E. Levy, Minneapolis: University of Minnesota Press, 2007, p. 9.

"Our need for money . . .": César Chávez, Levy, p. 15.

"the fattest cats . . .": Ibid.

"For each tail . . .": Ibid.

"It was my mother . . .": César Chávez, Ibid., p. 25.

"would offer to do . . .": César Chávez, Ibid., pp. 25–26.

"Since those days . . .": César Chávez, Ibid., p. 27.

"who plowed the land . . .": César Chávez, Ibid., p. 40.

"God writes in . . .": César Chávez, Ibid., p. 42.

"I didn't learn . . ." : Juana Chávez, as remembered by César Chávez, Ibid., p. 65.

"school was just . . .": César Chávez, Ibid.

"didn't affect the . . .": César Chávez, Ibid., p. 82.

"César used to . . .": Helen Chávez, Ibid., p. 87.

"the worst of my . . .": César Chávez, Ibid., p. 84.

"The braceros took all . . .": César Chávez, Ibid., p. 87.

"César had always . . .": Helen Chávez, Ibid., p. 147.

"My only hope . . .": César Chávez, Ibid.

CHAPTER 3   page 44

"The power of the . . .": César Chávez, Ibid., p. 151.

"I just drove by . . .": César Chávez, Ibid., p. 158.

"I was picking grapes . . .": Helen Chávez, Ibid.

"Red and black flags . . .": César Chávez, Ibid., p. 173.

CHAPTER 4   page 52

"I thought the growers . . .": César Chávez, Ibid., p. 183.

"*Sí!*": César Chávez, Ibid., p. 185.

"There is no interest . . .": Joseph G. Brosmer, "Spreading Strike Hits State's Grape Harvest," by Harry Bernstein, *Los Angeles Times*, September 21, 1965.

"We were told . . .": Rev. George Spindt, "Grape Strike Parley Urged by Churches," by Harry Bernstein, *Los Angeles Times*, September 29, 1965.

"condone the fact . . .": "An Open Letter to My Fellow Farmers," by Frederick Van Dyke, Van Dyke ranch, Stockton, California, July 12, 1959, Archives of Labor and Urban Affairs, Walter P. Reuther Library.

"imported laborers . . .": Ibid.

"benefit . . . agriculture . . .": Ibid.

"the excluded Americans.": James P. Mitchell, press release, CBS News, November 18, 1960, Archives of Labor and Urban Affairs, Walter P. Reuther Library.

"We used to own . . .": anonymous speaker, "Harvest of Shame" (documentary), by Edward R. Murrow, *CBS Reports*, 1960.

"roving picket lines . . .": student recruitment flyer, National Farm Workers Association, Archives of Labor and Urban Affairs, Walter P. Reuther Library.

"The best way . . .": César Chávez, Levy, p. 183.

"An event that . . .": Pete Velasco, "Events O'Day," personal notes, Archives of Labor and Urban Affairs, Walter P. Reuther Library.

"looked a lot . . .": Marshall Ganz, *The Fight in the Fields* (documentary film), Telles and Tejada-Flores.

"The history of AWOC . . .": Pete Velasco, "Events O'Day," January 15, 1966.

"side-swiping the . . .": Ibid.

"I think they're used . . .": anonymous speaker, *The Fight in the Fields* (documentary film), Telles and Tejada-Flores.

"We have no labor . . .": Ibid.

"our . . . workers.": Ibid.

"Chávez possibly has a . . ." and "reportedly . . .": FBI file, 1 of 7, Federal Bureau of Investigation, "Cesar Chavez & United Farm Workers et al," p. 4.

"several other individuals . . .": Ibid.

"a recent issue . . .": Ibid.

"Chávez told him . . .": Ibid., p. 10.

"the word 'HUELGA' . . .": Ibid.

"no subversive . . .": Ibid., p. 20.

"actual subversive . . .": Ibid., p. 22.

"a 'clean' background." : Ibid., p. 10.

"It makes the injustice . . .": Wayne "Chris" Hartmire, "34 Arrested in Grape Strike Plead Innocent," by Harry Bernstein, *Los Angeles Times*, October 21, 1965.

"no longer . . .": Loren Fote, Ibid.

"Sixty-seven hundred . . .": César Chávez, Levy, p. 193.

"As I was . . .": Edgar J. Gallardo, undated affidavit, Archives of Labor and Urban Affairs, Walter P. Reuther Library.

"Don't you ever . . .": César Chávez, Levy, p. 202.

"I am sure . . .": Bill Kircher, *The Fight in the Fields* (documentary film), Telles and Tejada-Flores.

"The growers cannot win . . .": Walter Reuther, "Reuther Pledges Union Help to Grape Strikers," by Harry Bernstein, *Los Angeles Times*, December 17, 1965.

"Fine, let's go . . .": Walter Reuther, as quoted by César Chávez, *The Fight in the Fields* (documentary film), Telles and Tejada- Flores.

"Well, I don't think . . .": César Chávez, Ibid.

CHAPTER 5 page 74

"[Robert Kennedy] came . . .": César Chávez, "César Chávez Oral History Interview—RFK, 1/28/1970" (transcript), interviewed by Dennis J. O'Brien at Delano, California, John F. Kennedy Presidential Library and Museum, p. 5.

"Senator Murphy was . . .": Ibid., pp. 4–5.

"In the midst . . .": Ibid., p. 5.

"to please give . . .": Ibid., p. 6.

"had enough . . .": Ibid., p. 5.

"that no one could . . .": unnamed source, "2 Senators Term Farm Housing in Tulare 'Shameful'," by Harry Bernstein, *Los Angeles Times*, March 16, 1966.

"If we can put . . .": Robert Kennedy, Ibid.

"Well, if . . . somebody . . .": Leroy Galyen and Robert Kennedy exchange, *The Fight in the Fields* (documentary film), Telles and Tejada-Flores.

"Senator Kennedy was like . . .": César Chávez, "César Chávez Oral History Interview—RFK, 1/28/1970," p. 5.

"The consumer boycott . . .": "The Grape Boycott . . . Why It Has to Be," by César Chávez, *El Malcriado* (undated), Archives of Labor and Urban Affairs, Walter P. Reuther Library.

"pilgrimage of a . . .": César Chávez, "Protest March for Farm Labor Gets Under Way," by Harry Bernstein, *Los Angeles Times*, March 18, 1966.

"the 'Table Grape King'": *Delano Grapevine* (undated), Archives of Labor and Urban Affairs, Walter P. Reuther Library.

"by more than 75%.": Ibid.

"the theme of the march . . .": César Chávez, "Protest March for Farm Labor Gets Under Way," Bernstein, March 18, 1966.

"also a march . . .": Ibid.

"Talk to me . . .": César Chávez, Levy, p. 216.

"Labor history . . .": Bill Kircher, "Schenley to Bargain with a Grape Union," by Peter Bart, *New York Times*, April 7, 1966.

"the Council of . . .": Ibid.

"We are no longer . . .": Dolores Huerta, "Grape Strikers Score Gov. Brown as March Ends," by Lawrence E. Davies, *New York Times*, April 11, 1966.

"We look forward . . .": Bill Kircher, "Grape Grower to Recognize Union," by Richard West, *Los Angeles Times*, April 7, 1966.

"We realize . . .": César Chávez. Ibid.

"as fast as . . .": Dolores Huerta, Levy, p. 225.

"Di Giorgio Corporation urges . . .": Robert Di Giorgio, letter to Larry Itliong, April 6, 1966, Archives of Labor and Urban Affairs, Walter P. Reuther Library.

"all parties to cooperate . . .": Governor Edmund G. Brown, press release, April 8, 1966, Archives of Labor and Urban Affairs, Walter P. Reuther Library.

"good offices . . .": Ibid.

"the mutually . . .": Ibid.

"The boycott . . . began . . .": César Chávez, Levy, p. 223.

CHAPTER 6 page 88

"Mr. Ceasar Mosquito . . .": R. L. Myer, letter to employees of Sierra Vista ranch, June 4, 1966, Archives of Labor and Urban Affairs, Walter P. Reuther Library.

"raise no more . . .": Ibid.

"many jobs . . .": Ibid.

"They feel that . . .": "Rio Grande's Farm Labor Drama Depresses Senators," by Robin Lloyd, *Washington Post*, July 9, 1967.

"now is . . ." and "all we want . . .": "Today in History: Chicano Farmworkers Begin Strike," by Hillary Sorin, *Houston Chronicle* (Chron.com), June 1, 2010, blog.chron.com/txpotomac/2010/06/today-in-texas-history-chicano-farm-workers-begin-strike/ (accessed September 6, 2013).

"that require[d] . . .": "Rio Grande's Farm Labor Drama Depresses Senators," Lloyd, July 9, 1967.

"The Rangers have . . .": Bill Kircher, "Texas Rangers Beat Leaders, Union Says," by the Associated Press, *Washington Post*, July 5, 1967.

"hired strikebreakers.": U.S. senator Ralph Yarborough, "Rio Grande's Farm Labor Drama Depresses Senators," Lloyd, July 9, 1967.

"Hell, I wouldn't . . ." and "Those people . . .": Captain A. Y. Allee, "Texas Ranger Not a Hero to All," by John Kifner, *New York Times*, March 23, 1970.

"If there is no . . .": "Farm Workers in Texas End Two-Month March," by Martin Waldron, *New York Times*, September 5, 1966.

"a gray burro . . .": Ibid.

"sympathized with . . .": Ibid.

"a slap in the face . . .": Father Sherrill Smith, "Farm Workers in Texas End Two-Month March," Waldron, September 5, 1966.

"that he was prevented . . .": *El Malcriado* (undated), p. 23.

"Magdaleno Dimas . . .": Jerry Cohen, Levy, p. 451.

"was attracted by . . .": "Carmel Valley's Jerry Cohen Led the UFW's Legal Struggle until a Falling-Out Over Strategy," by Zachary Stahl, *Monterey County Weekly*, October 22, 2009, montereycountyweekly.com/news/cover/article_2776431b-99fa-5803-aaf4-f6f5d8777d52.html (accessed August 23, 2013).

"[Chávez] lied . . .": *Gringo Justice: The United Farm Workers Union, 1967–1981*, by Jerry Cohen, p. 5, amherst.edu/library/archives/holdings/electexts/cohen.

CHAPTER 7 page 100

"This is to verify . . .": César Chávez, letter to John Gardner, January 12, 1968, Archives of Labor and Urban Affairs, Walter P. Reuther Library.

"a short-cut . . .": César Chávez, "Farm Union Leader Chávez Fasts to Support Nonviolence," by Harry Bernstein, *Los Angeles Times*, February 25, 1968.

"We cannot build . . .": Ibid.

"The deliberate taking . . .": Ibid.

"to our commitment . . .": Ibid.

"If I kick . . .": Jerry Cohen, recalling Judge Walter Osborne's comments, Levy, p. 281. (Note: The citation credited to Osborne appears in other sources, but Harry Bernstein identifies Morton Barker as the Superior Court judge who postponed the hearing at length. "Judge Fears for Chávez' Health, Delays Hearing," *Los Angeles Times*, February 28, 1968.)

"the Senator got . . .": César Chávez, "César Chávez Oral History Interview—RFK, 1/28/1970" (transcript), p. 18.

CHAPTER 8 page 110

"Your kind words . . .": Bayard Rustin, letter to Dolores C. Huerta, April 26, 1968, Archives of Labor and Urban Affairs, Walter P. Reuther Library.

"With Senator . . .": César Chávez, "Chávez Oral History Interview—RFK, 1/28/1970" (transcript), p. 16.

"The farmer has . . .": Governor Ronald Reagan, "Farm Workers Jobless Plan Urged by Reagan," by Jerry Gillam, *Los Angeles Times*, December 4, 1968.

"benefits [would] increase . . .": Ibid.

"an incredible document . . .": Joe Gunterman, letter to César Chávez, December 4, 1968, Archives of Labor and Urban Affairs, Walter P. Reuther Library.

"to discuss the grape . . .": "Safeway Answers Consumer Appeals with Arrests," *El Malcriado*, May 1969, Archives of Labor and Urban Affairs, Walter P. Reuther Library.

"this argument was . . .": Ibid.

"that one of the principles . . .": "U.S. Fresh Grape Shipments to South Vietnam and Department of Defense Purchases of Table Grapes," United Farm Workers Organizing Committee, AFL-CIO, November 30, 1968, Archives of Labor and Urban Affairs, Walter P. Reuther Library.

"We think the Pentagon . . .": "Grape Boycott #2," by R. Peter Straus, president, Radio WMCA editorial, June 2–3, 1969, Archives of Labor and Urban Affairs, Walter P. Reuther Library.

"This industry . . .": Martin Zaninovich, "Most Vineyards Standing Firm, Leaders Claim," by Harry Bernstein, *Los Angeles Times*, June 17, 1969, Archives of Labor and Urban Affairs, Walter P. Reuther Library.

"the backing of . . .": César Chávez, Levy, p. 294.

"the Giumarras furnished . . .": Ibid.

"for a 'freeze'" : Senator Alan Cranston, letter to Mrs. Florence Klinger, July 17, 1969, Archives of Labor and Urban Affairs, Walter P. Reuther Library.

"On August 1st . . .": César Chávez, "Statement of César Chávez Before Senate Subcommittee on Migratory Labor, September 29, 1969" (transcript), Archives of Labor and Urban Affairs, Walter P. Reuther Library.

"[Their results] confirmed . . .": Ibid.

"An undisclosed number . . .": Ibid.

"She vomited . . .": Ibid.

"was engaged in . . .": Ibid.

"A boycott of . . .": Lionel Steinberg, Levy, p. 296.

"While before the strike . . .": Ibid.

"interested in . . .": Monsignor George Higgins, Levy, p. 305.

"I don't like . . .": Monsignor Roger Mahony, "First Grapes with Union Label Shipped to Market from Coast," by Steven V. Roberts, *New York Times*, May 31, 1970.

"It's dawned on . . .": Monsignor Roger Mahony, quoting John Giumarra Jr., "Grape Growers Accept Contract; Signing to Signal Boycott's End," by Bill Boyarsky and Harry Bernstein, *Los Angeles Times*, July 29, 1970.

"If it works here . . .": John Giumarra Jr., "Handshakes Seal Pact Ending Grape Boycott," by Bill Boyarsky, *Los Angeles Times*, July 30, 1970.

"This is the beginning . . .": César Chávez, Ibid.

"were surprised to see . . .": César Chávez, Ibid.

"The strikers, and . . .": César Chávez, "Farmworker Movement Documentation Project," oral history (transcript), compiled by LeRoy Chatfield, farmworkermovement.us (accessed July 9, 2013).

CHAPTER 9 page 128

"a stab in the back . . .": Larry Itliong, "Battle Between Teamsters and Chavez Looms," by Harry Bernstein, *Los Angeles Times*, August 5, 1970.

"No longer can . . .": César Chávez, Ibid.

"We in the top . . .": Larry Itliong, *The Fight in the Fields: Cesar Chavez and the Farmworkers Movement*, by Susan Ferriss and Ricardo Sandoval, Orlando, FL: Harcourt Brace (Paradigm Productions), 1997, p. 211.

"We lived with . . .": "Chávez Battles Ariz. Curb on Harvest Strikes," by Howard Armstrong, *Washington Post*, May 25, 1972.

"Sí se puede . . .": Ibid.

"His desire was . . .": "The Madness of Cesar Chavez," by Caitlin Flanagan, *The Atlantic*, June 13, 2011, theatlantic.com/magazine/archive/2011/07/the-madness-of-cesar-chavez/308557 (accessed August 5, 2013).

"Every time we look . . .": Ibid.

INDEX

Lettuce and vegetable growers called for bracero workers to harvest their struck fields. The cartoon depicts the way these foreign workers often were treated.

BRACEROS FOR SALINAS

A farm worker on a picket line calls out to strikebreakers working in the vineyards to join the strike in Delano, California, in 1966.

PICTURE CREDITS

Alamy/kolvenbach: endpapers.

AP Images: front jacket (right), 2, 19, 35, 126–127, 129, 148–149, 154–155.

Larry Dane Brimner: 28.

The Dolph Briscoe Center for American History, The University of Texas at Austin, Lee (Russell W.) Photograph Collection: 12–13, 40.

Guy Porfirio Illustration: 22.

The Image Works: © 1976 George Ballis/Take Stock: 4–5, 46–47, 170; © 1966 Ernest Lowe/Take Stock: 84–85.

Leonard Nadel Collection, Archives Center, National Museum of American History, Smithsonian Institution: 16.

Library of Congress, Prints and Photographs Division: LC-USF34-016200-E: front jacket (left), 150; LC-USF344-007485-ZB: 6–7; LC-USZ6-1018: 9; LC-USF34-016204-E: 10–11; LC-USZ62-56051: 26–27; LC-USZ62-132712: 31; LC-USZ6-1184: 33.

Magnum Photos, Paul Fusco: 52–53, 88–89.

Reprinted by arrangement with The Heirs to the Estate of Martin Luther King, Jr., c/o Writers House as agent for the proprietor, New York, NY. Copyright © 1968 Dr. Martin Luther King, Jr. Copyright © renewed 1996 Coretta Scott King: 112.

Courtesy of Dolores Velasco: 76.

Walter P. Reuther Library, AV Department: 14, 15, 21, 23, 34, 39, 42–43, 49, 54, 58, 61, 62, 68, 69, 70, 72–73, 74–75, 83, 90, 95, 99, 100–101, 102–103, 106–107, 108–109, 116–117, 121, 122, 125, 130, 135, 136, 138, 140, 142, 143, back jacket; *El Malcriado*: 24, 45, 50, 87, 111, 133, 157, 169.

For information about permission to
reproduce selections from this book,
please contact:
permissions@highlights.com.

Calkins Creek
An Imprint of Highlights
815 Church Street
Honesdale, Pennsylvania 18431

Printed in China

ISBN: 978-1-59078-997-1

Library of Congress Control Number:
2014935299

First edition

10 9 8 7 6 5 4 3 2 1

Designed by Bill Anton | Service Station
Production by Margaret Mosomillo

Titles set in ITC Cheltenham Book
and Boycott

Text set in ITC Cheltenham Book
and Univers LT Std 67 Bold Condensed

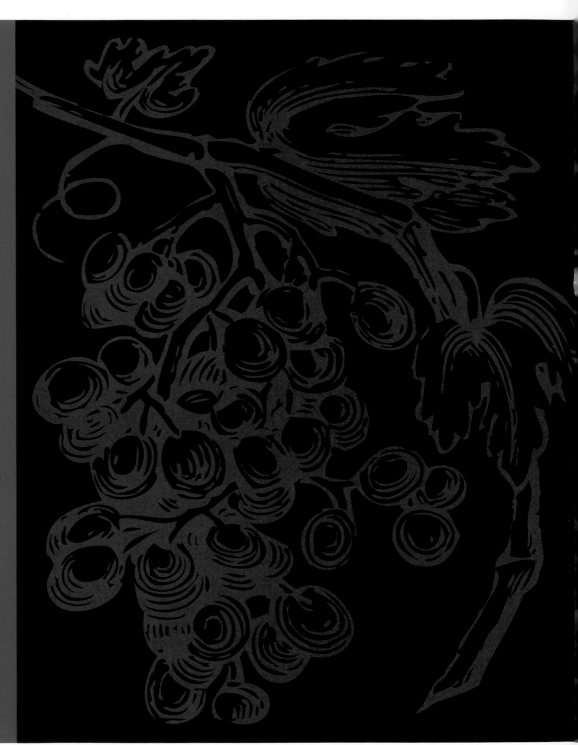